Encyclopedia
= of =
NORTH
AMERICAN
HISTORY

Encyclopedia
== of ==
NORTH
AMERICAN
HISTORY

6

Mackenzie's Explorations—North Pole Expeditions

John C. Super

Consulting Editor

Marshall Cavendish
New York • London • Toronto

Marshall Cavendish Corporation
99 White Plains Road
Tarrytown, New York 10591–9001

© Marshall Cavendish Corporation, 1999

Editor's note: Many systems of dating have been used by different cultures throughout history. The Encyclopedia of North American History uses B.C.E. (Before Common Era) and C.E. (Common Era) instead of B.C. (Before Christ) and A.D. (Anno Domini, "In the Year of Our Lord") out of respect for the diversity of the world's peoples.

Library of Congress Cataloging-in-Publication Data

Encyclopedia of North American history / consulting editor, John C. Super.
p.   cm.
Includes bibliographical references and index.
ISBN 0–7614–7084–0 (set : alk. paper)
1. North America—History—Encyclopedias. I. Super, John C., 1944–
E45.E49   1998
970'.003—dc21   97–33131
                                                 CIP

ISBN 0–7614–7084–0 (set)
ISBN 0–7614–7090–5 (vol. 6)

Printed in Malaysia
Bound in the U.S.A.

Contents

Mackenzie's Explorations

Sir Alexander Mackenzie, a Scottish fur trader, explorer, and businessman in North America, was born at Stornoway, on the island of Lewis, Scotland, about 1764. He emigrated to New York with his widowed father in 1774, but because of the American Revolution, he went to Montreal in 1778. In Montreal he joined a fur-trading company, Gregory, McLeod and Company, which merged with the North West Company in 1787. Mackenzie became a partner and was appointed to take charge of the North West Company trading post at Fort Chipewyan, Alberta, on Lake Athabasca in 1788. From this post on June 3, 1789, Mackenzie and a party of Canadians and a few Indian guides set out on a voyage to Great Slave Lake and down the river that now bears his name, hoping to reach the Pacific Ocean, but Mackenzie was disappointed to find that the river led north-northwest. On July 16, 1789, the company reached the river's delta at the Arctic Ocean. In a little over three months (102 days), Mackenzie had returned to Fort Chipewyan, having explored one of the four largest rivers (1,100 miles, or 1,770 kilometers, long) of North America, the Mackenzie.

In 1793 Mackenzie made a second important exploration. On May 9, 1793, his party of ten crossed the Rocky Mountains, ascending the Peace River and its tributary, the Parsnip. The company followed the Fraser River for part of its course and then pushed westward overland, following Indian trails to the Bella Coola River. Descending the Bella Coola, Mackenzie reached the Pacific Ocean at Dean Channel, near what is now British Columbia, on July 22, 1793. On August 24, 1793, Mackenzie and his company returned to Fort Fork on the Peace River. Mackenzie had become the first European to cross the continent north of Mexico. In 1801, his book *Voyage from Montreal on the River St. Lawrence, Through the Continent of North America to the Frozen and Pacific Oceans, in the Years 1789 and 1793* was published. Because of his successes and heroics, he was knighted by King George III in 1802.

Alvin K. Benson

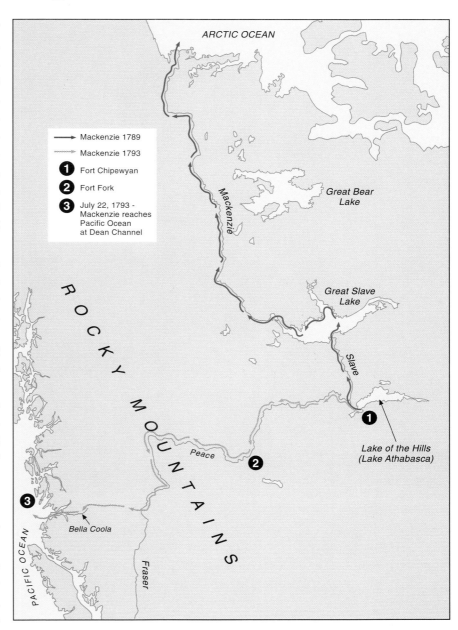

Legend:
- Mackenzie 1789
- Mackenzie 1793
1. Fort Chipewyan
2. Fort Fork
3. July 22, 1793 - Mackenzie reaches Pacific Ocean at Dean Channel

Alexander Mackenzie's two major expeditions opened up Canada for settlers.

CAUSES AND EFFECTS

Like other European explorers before him, Alexander Mackenzie wanted to find a route across North America to the Pacific Ocean and a Northwest Passage to lucrative trade with Asia. Mackenzie was the first European to cross the North American continent north of Mexico, preceding the journey of Meriwether Lewis and William Clark by more than ten years. Mackenzie's 1793 trip convinced him that searching for a Northwest Passage was useless, and he ultimately promoted the idea of conducting trade with Asia across the Pacific Ocean.

SEE ALSO: LEWIS & CLARK EXPEDITION.

Mackenzie's Ministry

Alexander Mackenzie introduced key legislation as prime minister of Canada in the 1870's.

CAUSES AND EFFECTS

Controversy and scandal implicating government officials and railroad company contributions led to the resignation of the Conservative Party as the governing party of Canada in 1873. The Liberal Party took office with Alexander Mackenzie as Canada's new prime minister.

His ineffective leadership, however, compounded with mounting economic difficulties during this period, resulted in a Conservative Party victory in the next parliamentary elections in 1878.

The Liberals did not again return to power in Ottawa for nearly two decades.

Scottish-born Alexander Mackenzie emigrated to Canada in 1842. Considered an honest and dedicated individual, he took the leadership of the Liberal Party in 1867 and on November 5, 1873, became Canada's second prime minister after the Pacific Scandal ended years of Conservative Party rule (SEE Macdonald's Ministry). The parliamentary elections of 1874 gave a sizable Liberal Party majority to support Canada's new prime minister.

Mackenzie hoped to stabilize Canada's economy by shifting priorities away from a costly transcontinental railroad project of the former administration in favor of less ambitious schemes (SEE Canadian Pacific Railway). Unfortunately, Canada began to experience a severe economic depression shortly after he took office. Mounting problems weakened his ability to govern, and the railroad controversy continued.

Canada's relationship with the United States was uneven. Trade proposals with the United States were rejected by the Americans in 1874. In addition, the Mackenzie administration increased tariffs on foreign imports. Strained relations with Britain, Canada's former colonial owner, also created difficulties for Mackenzie, who defended the independence of his adopted homeland. Domestically, the new province of British Columbia complained of its treatment by the federal authorities in Ottawa. Having joined the Dominion of Canada in 1871, it threatened to withdraw unless prior commitments made to it were fulfilled.

Under Mackenzie's leadership, several noteworthy achievements occurred. Voting by secret ballot became law. The Supreme Court of Canada, the highest court in the nation, was created in 1875. Legislation to deal with political corruption was adopted. The government established the Royal Military College at Kingston, Ontario, to train Canadian army officers. In addition, Canada's famous Mounted Police, first named the North-West Mounted Police and later renamed the Royal Canadian Mounted Police, began their activities in 1874 (SEE Royal Canadian Mounted Police). The Mackenzie government provided training and support for the maintenance of law and order in the western regions of Canada.

Economic problems, and growing disarray in the Liberal Party, led to a sweeping Liberal defeat in the 1878 parliamentary elections, ending Mackenzie's ministry on October 9. The Conservative Party returned to power, under John A. Macdonald. Mackenzie continued as Liberal leader for two years, before retiring from politics. He died in 1892.

Taylor Stults

SEE ALSO: CANADIAN PACIFIC RAILWAY; CANADIAN POLITICAL PARTIES; MACDONALD'S MINISTRIES; ROYAL CANADIAN MOUNTED POLICE.

McKinley's Presidency

On November 3, 1896, voters turned out in record numbers, giving 50 percent of their vote to William McKinley, former Republican governor of Ohio and twice-elected congressman. His main claim to fame was the McKinley Tariff (1890), which raised protection rates to record heights. McKinley's campaign consisted of walking to his front porch in Canton, Ohio, and addressing trainload after trainload of visitors brought by the railroads to hear him speak.

The real campaign, however, was fought in a Republican-dominated press and in tens of millions of pieces of campaign literature designed to influence the votes of urban workers. Due to large contributions from industrialists and financiers, along with the efforts of Marcus Hanna, who, on the basis of his successes as Ohio political party boss, created a political machine to organize the Republican Party, McKinley did not have to leave his front porch for his message to travel far and wide.

McKinley's opponent on the Democratic and Populist ballot, William Jennings Bryan, carried his campaign more than 18,000 miles, or 28,962 kilometers, to twenty-one states, addressing in the process more than five million people. To some he appeared to be a crusading prophet or people's savior, to others a dynamic salesperson using modern merchandising techniques. The campaign revolved around economic issues such as whether to increase the post-depression money supply through "free silver" and an imperialist versus a more isolationist foreign policy. Bryan's pro-silver, low-tariff, and anti-annexationist appeal gained him only a respectable 46 percent of the vote. Bryan did not carry a single urban or industrial state.

DOMESTIC AFFAIRS

McKinley became chief executive of a United States still reeling from the effects of the Panic of 1893 and the worst depression it had ever experienced. The March of Coxey's Army and the Pullman Strike threatened to be merely two in a continuing series of national traumas (SEE Pullman Strike).

William McKinley won two presidential elections, in 1896 and 1900. In 1896 he conducted his campaign from his front porch.

During 1894 paper-money holders traded their dollars for gold, and foreign investors cashed their American securities, causing gold to cross the Atlantic. The money situation had reached crisis proportions, a fact symbolized by banking magnate J. P. Morgan's $62 million loan to the government to pump new financial blood into the system. In his inaugural address, McKinley issued the oxymoron to "make haste slowly." His dictum to Congress was "Legislation helpful to producers is helpful to all."

SUMMARY

➤ In 1896, Republican William McKinley was elected president, earning 50 percent of the vote to defeat Democrat and Populist William Jennings Bryan.
➤ He reluctantly entered into a war with Spain in 1898, which resulted in the United States' becoming a world power.
➤ He was reelected in a landslide victory over Bryan in 1900 but was shot by an anarchist in 1901 and died of gangrene in a week.

VIEWPOINTS

BRYAN'S CROSS OF GOLD SPEECH

The Panic of 1893, followed by the nation's worst depression to date, led the two major political parties to confront the most pressing issue of the day: the national money supply. The money issue was already catapulting a new party, the Populists, to great popularity with debt-ridden farmers in the South and West.

At the 1896 Democratic National Convention in Chicago, three speakers favored the gold standard and three favored free coinage of silver. The situation provided a golden opportunity for William Jennings Bryan, the thirty-six-year-old two-term congressman from Nebraska who had made his reputation as the "boy orator of Platte," to give the most powerful speech of any U.S. political campaign: "If they dare to come out in the open and defend the gold standard as a good thing, we will fight . . . their demand for a gold standard by saying to them 'You shall not press down upon the brow of labor this crown of thorns; you shall not crucify mankind on a cross of gold.'"

He ended with his arms outstretched in imitation of the crucifixion, and electrified delegates rose to a thunderous ovation. Bryan won the Democratic nomination from the incumbent Grover Cleveland on the fifth ballot and the following month he was selected as the Populist candidate at the party's St. Louis convention. The election of 1896 became one of gold versus silver.

A cartoon from the 1900 presidential election has William Jennings Bryan blowing up "imperialist windbag" McKinley. Under McKinley, the United States began to acquire colonies and become an imperial power.

As McKinley took office, fortuitous events began to occur. New mining techniques and the discovery of huge gold deposits in Alaska, South Africa, and Australia rapidly increased the bullion supply. In 1900 McKinley made gold the only standard of currency with the Gold Standard Act. Crop failures in Europe caused high demand for U.S. grain, driving up prices and creating prosperity for farmers.

Industrialists were overjoyed by the election of McKinley and buoyed by his support of the highly protectionist Dingley Tariff (1897). Moreover, it was clear that the depression had long since bottomed out. Renewed confidence caused industrial expansion, a rise in the stock market, and an end to unemployment.

FOREIGN AFFAIRS

Although proannexationist regarding Hawaii, McKinley, like President Grover Cleveland before him, was opposed to intervention in Cuba. During his presidency, McKinley remained hesitant about active involvement in foreign affairs. Spain's suppression of the Cuban revolution grew tighter. McKinley offered several times to buy Cuba and land for the building of a canal in Panama, but his offers were refused. The explosion of the U.S. ship *Maine*, most likely an accident of spontaneous combustion, produced an outburst of nationalist rage and demands for revenge against the presumed sabotage. McKinley did his best to temper the jingoist frenzy, urging a calm investigation of the circumstances of the sinking.

McKinley ordered, on April 22, 1898, a naval blockade of Cuba. Within forty-eight hours, Spain declared war on the United States (SEE Spanish-American War). From the military standpoint, actions in Cuba and the Philippines, also held by Spain, were successful beyond belief, bringing an end to hostilities in three months. McKinley followed military actions from a war room, filled with state-of-the-art communications equipment, set up in the White House. He could now bask in the glow of his rapid victory in his role as commander in chief.

Under the terms of the peace treaty, Spain turned over control of Cuba, which would be occupied by the U.S. military, and relinquished Puerto Rico and the Philippines to U.S. annexation. Although Hawaii was not connected to the war in any way, those islands were also annexed. McKinley became chief executive of an empire.

The events of 1898 altered the president's role. McKinley now used special war powers to administer Puerto Rico and Cuba. He also sent a force of 20,000 to the Philippines to suppress a guerrilla movement led by former U.S. ally Emilio Aguinaldo, who naively believed that the war had been about gaining

independence for Filipinos. In 1900, without asking Congress, McKinley sent U.S. forces to China to join other major powers in crushing the Boxer Rebellion. The previous year, he had twice demanded the establishment of an Open Door Policy in China, which would

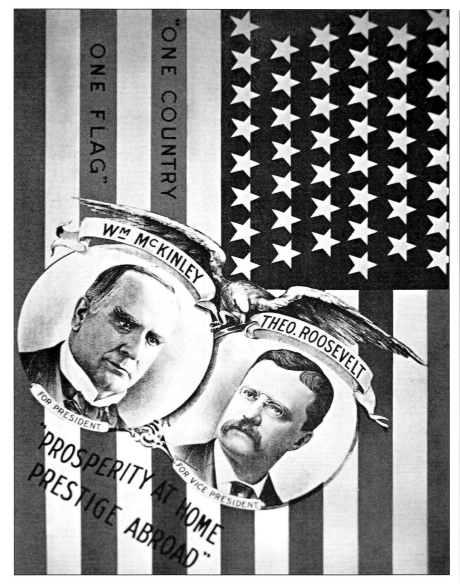

A 1900 election poster promotes William McKinley for reelection as president with Theodore Roosevelt as his vice president.

CAUSES AND EFFECTS

William McKinley was chosen as the Republican candidate in the election of 1896 to defend protective tariff and hard-money policies supported by industrial interests. His nomination and subsequent election were skillfully orchestrated by Marcus A. Hanna. An industrialist and Ohio political boss, Hanna raised huge sums to launch a newspaper campaign blitz.

Industrialists gave freely to prevent policy changes arising from the Panic of 1893, which had prompted the nation's worst depression to date. McKinley's election was a turning point in U.S. politics. It led to professional political party managers who ran efficient organizations that were fueled by large financial backers and could spend freely on mass media to influence the electorate. Rapid economic recovery took place after 1896. A short, victorious war against Spain in 1898 caused the United States to become an imperial power with a world role. McKinley's successful administration led to Republican domination of national politics until 1932 (except for 1913–1921, when Woodrow Wilson served as president).

President McKinley is shot by the anarchist Leon Czolgosz on September 6, 1901, at the Pan-American Exposition in Buffalo, New York. McKinley died in the hospital a week later. His doctors had been unable to locate the bullet inside his body and he died after gangrene set in.

allow American companies to have the same trading rights as the major powers in their respective spheres of influence in China. The Open Door Policy was added to the Monroe Doctrine as a basic operating principle for U.S. foreign policy.

THE ELECTION OF 1900

As the election of 1900 approached, reports circulated about the less glorious aspects of the war. Contaminated food, poor sanitation, and incompetent medical care took a terrible toll not only in the war but also at military bases at home. Treatment of African-American soldiers, who had played a major part in winning the war, was equally horrid. Though he issued some symbolic compliments about African-American soldiers, McKinley was intent on drawing white Southern support away from Bryan's Democrats in the next election.

In answer to attacks by the Anti-Imperialist League on the hypocrisy of a nation that had gained its freedom from a colonial power becoming a colonial power and depriving others of their freedom, McKinley made the dynamic war hero and former governor of New York, Theodore Roosevelt, his running mate. McKinley did not campaign in the election. Bryan had added anti-imperialism to his anti-gold-standard and antiprotectionism platform but could do little to offset public perceptions of national glory and prosperity. With Prosperity at Home, Prestige Abroad as his campaign slogan, McKinley won in a landslide, exceeding his 1896 popular vote by 100,000 and his electoral college vote by 21.

THE SECOND ADMINISTRATION

In the first months of his new administration, McKinley focused on the plan to build a canal in Panama and on the formulation of reciprocity agreements for a tariff agreement that would serve the changed needs of a successful industrial and imperial nation (SEE Panama Canal). He also began to nudge his party toward regulation of the nation's large industries, some of which had grown to monopolistic proportions (SEE Antitrust Laws). On September 6, 1901, while McKinley was greeting the public at the Pan-American Exposition in Buffalo, New York, an anarchist, Leon Czolgosz, stepped forward and fired two shots from a revolver. One shot ripped through McKinley's stomach, and though he lingered for over a week, the gangrene produced along the path of the bullet, still lodged in his body, proved fatal. He died on September 14, and Roosevelt became president.

McKinley's passing was sincerely mourned by the nation. During his administration, the presidency and the nation assumed a more dynamic character. Recent studies of McKinley have labeled him a reticent expansionist and the first modern president. Others view him as the last in a line of unimaginative and traditional Civil War veterans who became president. In either case, he was a leader at a time of important changes, if not a leader of these changes.

Irwin Halfond

TEMPER OF THE TIMES

THE TARIFF QUESTION

Though Republicans generally favored high protective tariffs (taxes imposed on imported goods), Democrats believed in lower tariffs to stimulate competition and thereby lower prices for industrial products. Presidents Chester Arthur and Grover Cleveland had tried, with little success, to reduce tariff rates.

While he was a congressman, the protective tariff was William McKinley's pet issue. He firmly believed that high tariffs stimulated industrial growth, created new jobs, and fostered general prosperity. Among his few special talents, McKinley was considered to be the only congressman "who could make reading a tariff schedule sound like poetry." The 1890 McKinley Tariff, which created a high protective tariff, first helped his political star rise by attracting support from Eastern financial interests.

During the election campaign of 1896, William Jennings Bryan and the Democrats embraced the Populist platform of lowering tariffs, while McKinley and the Republicans remained solidly protectionist. In the first year of his presidency, McKinley actively supported the Dingley Tariff (1897), which raised import duties an average 52 percent, creating an all-time high for protectionism.

Following the victorious Spanish-American War in 1898, the United States became a more confident industrial power and a world power, and the federal government gained an opportunity to play a larger role. Bumper crops in the United States and food shortages in Europe also meant high demand for U.S. grain. Business began to feel that high tariffs no longer served its interests. By the beginning of his second administration, even McKinley began to doubt that high tariffs served the national interest. However, an assassin's bullet cut short any attempt by McKinley to lower tariff rates by comprehensive reciprocal agreements.

SEE ALSO:
PANAMA CANAL;
RECIPROCITY TREATY;
SPANISH-AMERICAN
WAR.

FURTHER READING

• Coletta, Paolo, ed. *Threshold to American Internationalism: Essays on the Foreign Policy of William McKinley.* New York: Exposition Press, 1970.
• Dobson, John. *Reticent Expansionism: The Foreign Policy of William McKinley.* Pittsburgh: Duquesne University Press, 1988.
• Glad, Paul. *McKinley, Bryan, and the People.* Philadelphia: J. B. Lippincott, 1964.
• Gould, Lewis L. *The Presidency of William McKinley.* Lawrence: Regents Press of Kansas, 1980.
• Morgan, H. Wayne. *William McKinley and His America.* Syracuse, N.Y.: Syracuse University Press, 1963.

President McKinley is portrayed as a heavyweight in a cartoon depiction of his fight with "lightweight" free-trade advocates in the battle over tariffs.

Malcolm X's Assassination

A police officer clears the way as the body of Malcolm X, the African-American leader of the Nation of Islam, is carried from the Audubon Ballroom, New York City, after he had been assassinated there on February 21, 1965.

CAUSES AND EFFECTS

Extreme tensions in the 1960's developed between Malcolm X and Nation of Islam leader Elijah Muhammad. Other Black Muslims considered Malcolm a threat to their movement. Following Malcolm's death, many African-Americans, disillusioned with the lack of progress in the Civil Rights movement, turned to the ideology of the black power movement. This trend was especially noticeable in the Student Nonviolent Coordinating Committee and the Congress of Racial Equality.

SEE ALSO:
CHICAGO RIOTS; CIVIL RIGHTS MOVEMENT; DETROIT RIOTS; KING'S ASSASSINATION; LONG, HOT SUMMER; MARCH ON WASHINGTON; WATTS RIOT.

In the late 1940's, Malcolm Little, a young African-American who was serving a prison sentence for burglary, met Elijah Muhammad, leader of the Nation of Islam, who preached that the white man was the devil. Little soon became a Black Muslim, taking the name Malcolm X.

By the mid-1960's, many African-Americans were disappointed because the Civil Rights movement had accomplished very little (SEE Civil Rights Movement). They turned to Malcolm, who advocated meeting violence with violence and working without whites as the only means to power. Malcolm's popularity soon eclipsed that of Muhammad, who then forced Malcolm out of the Nation of Islam. By 1964, Malcolm was still preaching that blacks should help themselves, but he was no longer verbally attacking all white Americans as the devil. He saved his rage for white supremacists. By the spring of 1965, Malcolm had made enough enemies that he feared for his life. In particular, tensions between him and the Black Muslims had worsened.

On February 21, 1965, Malcolm held a mass meeting at the Audubon Ballroom in the Harlem section of New York City. The normally impassioned, energetic man looked exhausted. Malcolm began to speak to the crowd of a few hundred. Then, near the middle of the room, two men began a diversionary fight while another rushed toward the podium with a shotgun. Malcolm, who may never have seen his assassin, tried to quiet the crowd. The man with the shotgun fired at least a dozen pellets into Malcolm's chest from fifteen feet away. The two men who had been staging a fight followed the shotgun blast with several rounds from their revolvers. During the chaos, two of the three assailants escaped. Malcolm was dead.

Several months later, police caught the two suspects who had fled. All three of those apprehended were Black Muslims. Some people suspected Muhammad was behind the killing. Others believed a larger conspiracy had been behind Malcolm's death. Black nationalists had lost their greatest leader, but his death sparked more interest in the black-power movement that emphasized African-Americans gaining power through violence. His assassination also illustrated the divisions that existed within the African-American community. Such divisions contributed to the unraveling of the Civil Rights movement before the end of the decade.

Stephen A. Berrey

Manhattan Island Sale

The purchase of the island of Manhattan by the Dutch on May 6, 1626, was an unplanned and somewhat mistaken venture. The Dutch had claimed the coast of North America from Delaware north to Hudson Bay after Henry Hudson explored this area in search of a water route to India and China (SEE Hudson Bay Explorations) and had been trading with the native Americans in the region for valuable animal skins—beaver, bear, and otter—for more than a dozen years. They had established a number of forts to facilitate trade in this far-flung territory. In the spring of 1626, Dutch traders became caught in a war between the Mohawk and Mohegan, and several were killed (SEE Iroquois Confederacy). Peter Minuit, newly appointed director of the Dutch colony of New Amsterdam, arrived in early May to find a somewhat explosive situation, which he diffused with a two-part solution.

First, he purchased the whole of the wooded island of Manhattan from the Canarsee tribe, who were in the area but had no real claim to the land. Minuit paid them very little, perhaps a few minted coins but mostly with knives, woolen blankets, and other manufactured goods. Next, he moved settlers from outlying areas to the southernmost tip of the island, establishing the fortified settlement of New Amsterdam, which would become the focal point of the Dutch presence. This latter action would require that Minuit correct his earlier mistake by bringing together all of the tribes with a claim to the land and paying them as well.

Kelley Graham

Peter Minuit presents the Canarsee tribe of Manhattan Island with goods worth only a few Dutch guilders. In return the Indians agreed to Holland having rights of ownership to the island.

CAUSES AND EFFECTS

Dutch activity in the New World made up only a small part of the nation's seventeenth-century trade ventures. Nevertheless, by the early 1600's, the Dutch claimed a large portion of the coast of North America, from Delaware to the Hudson Bay.

In 1621, the West India Company was granted a monopoly on the fur trade from the head of the Delaware River to the Connecticut River Valley and established three trading posts. To ensure the colony's security and legitimize their claim to the area, the Dutch purchased Manhattan and established New Amsterdam as its center.

SEE ALSO: HUDSON BAY EXPLORATIONS; HUDSON'S BAY COMPANY; IROQUOIS CONFEDERACY.

March on Washington

Demonstrators in favor of reforming civil-rights laws arrive in Washington, D.C., at the conclusion of their march in 1963.

SUMMARY

➤ In August 1963, African-American leaders organized a civil-rights march on the nation's capital.
➤ The march, which had President Kennedy's support, brought together six major civil-rights organizations.
➤ Although speeches delivered to the assembled marchers stirred controversy, Martin Luther King, Jr., articulated a new American Dream of racial equality.

The civil rights movements of the 1950's, 1960's, and 1970's have been characterized as the greatest struggle for constitutional rights championed by oppressed groups in the history of the United States. Various nonviolent strategies, including sit-ins, boycotts, and mass demonstrations, were used to challenge the American social structure, which systematically disadvantaged women and people of color. The 1963 March on Washington, a mass demonstration in support of civil rights of African-Americans, represents one of the most significant events of the era.

PRELUDE TO THE MARCH

Bayard Rustin, the unofficial organizer of the march, convened a meeting in Washington, D.C., with march coordinators, the local police, and representatives from the Kennedy administration to examine potential logistical concerns. The primary concern was the possibility of disciplinary problems among some of the participants, especially those who advocated a more forceful protest. Rustin emphasized that there would be no disturbances and that a sizable number of African-American police officers would come in from New York to serve as parade marshals. He also explained that any potential lobbying activities would be monitored by march leaders.

President John F. Kennedy was concerned about the passage of his civil-rights bill. He believed he would need the support of Midwestern Republicans who took little interest in racial issues and would not be swayed by a mass demonstration in the nation's capital. Kennedy felt that if violence occurred during the march, it could negatively affect his bill. However, assurances given to him by the leaders of the march paved the way for his public endorsement of the march.

MAJOR CIVIL-RIGHTS GROUPS

The six major civil-rights organizations endorsed and participated in the march, but the outward show of unity belied the tensions that actually surrounded the event. A. Philip Randolph of the Negro American Labor Council (NALC), the official organizer of the march, was responsible for contacting the expected participants. He contacted Martin Luther King, Jr., of the Southern Christian Leadership Conference (SCLC), Roy Wilkins of the National Association for the Advancement of Colored People (NAACP), Whitney Young of the Urban League (UL), James Farmer of the Congress of Racial Equality (CORE), and John Lewis of the Student Nonviolent Coordinating Committee (SNCC).

Wilkins and Young were not very receptive of Randolph's plan. They said they were sympathetic with the intent of the protest; however, they feared that participating in such a march might damage their relationships with federal officials. They also expressed concern that their participation might jeopardize the financial support that both organizations received from liberal whites if violence erupted during the march.

THE MARCH

Rustin compiled detailed plans on the purpose and focus of the march. Among the more important components of the plan were calls for more and better jobs, a Fair Employment Practices Commission, and an increase in the minimum wage. The passage of the civil-rights bill was not one of Rustin's primary concerns.

The orderly, nonviolent march was the greatest show of integrated support for civil rights in the history of the nation's capital. The march took place August 28, 1963, with the leaders of the six major civil-rights organizations NALC, NAACP, SCLC, UL, CORE, and SNCC walking at the head of the demonstration.

The participants walked from the Washington Monument to the Lincoln Memorial, where each of the leaders addressed the assemblage. Other notable personalities were also given an opportunity to speak. Each speaker was supposed to have a speech prepared the day before for distribution to the press, and this requirement spawned two controversies.

African-American writer James Baldwin was denied the opportunity to deliver his speech as it was written. Rather than alter his speech, Baldwin chose to withdraw from the program. His speech, with modifications, was delivered by actor Burt Lancaster.

CAUSES AND EFFECTS

Martin Luther King, Jr., along with other civil-rights leaders, felt that U.S. president John F. Kennedy had not kept many of his campaign promises to the African-American community.

Kennedy had failed, for example, to issue an executive order outlawing segregation in public facilities. King and his fellow leaders therefore viewed the proposed March on Washington as a means of pressuring congressional action on pending civil-rights legislation. The march accomplished two important goals: It put the plight of African-Americans squarely before the American public, and it took a positive step toward increasing white participation in the Civil Rights movement.

Civil-rights leaders, including Martin Luther King, Jr. (second from left), meet with President John F. Kennedy (fourth from right) and Vice President Lyndon Johnson (third from right) in the Oval Office in 1963 to discuss the march on Washington.

TEMPER OF THE TIMES

KING'S "I HAVE A DREAM" SPEECH

The "I Have a Dream" speech that Martin Luther King, Jr., delivered at the 1963 March on Washington is one of the most powerful speeches in the history of the Civil Rights movement. It was not, however, composed entirely for the occasion. Parts of the speech were extracted from previous speeches. King had used the "dream" excerpt in Detroit, Michigan, and Birmingham, Alabama, in June 1963. The phrase "let freedom ring" had been used on a number of occasions, as far back as in 1956. He had given a number of speeches emphasizing the American Dream, which was a powerful symbol used to point out the contradictions between the opportunities for whites and blacks in the United States.

The text of King's speech is often reduced to the most famous part, in which he called for people to be judged by the "content of their character" and not by the color of their skin. The focal point of the speech, however, actually was the mistreatment of African-Americans. He used the metaphor of the "bad check" to symbolize everything established in the Constitution yet denied to African-Americans.

The "dream" symbolized the undying faith that African-Americans continued to embrace despite the different status accorded them because of their race. The speech elevated King's status as the central leader of the Civil Rights movement to new heights and is credited with much of the success of the Civil Rights movement itself.

Martin Luther King, Jr., makes his impassioned "I Have a Dream" speech in Washington in 1963.

SEE ALSO:
CIVIL RIGHTS
MOVEMENT.

FURTHER READING
•Cone, James H. *Martin and Malcolm and America: A Dream or a Nightmare?* Maryknoll, N.Y.: Orbis Books, 1991.
•Franklin, John Hope, and Isidore Starr. *The Negro America: A Reader on the Struggle for Civil Rights.* New York: Vintage Books, 1967.
•Garrow, David J. *Bearing the Cross: Martin Luther King, Jr., and the Southern Christian Leadership Conference.* New York: William Morrow, 1986.
•Witherspoon, William R. *Martin Luther King, Jr.: To the Mountaintop.* New York: Doubleday Press, 1985.

The other controversy involved Lewis, the SNCC chairperson. Three specific areas in Lewis' speech were found to be objectionable. First, Lewis indicated that SNCC could not endorse the president's civil-rights bill because it was too little, too late. Second, Lewis attacked the Kennedy administration for its lack of action in protecting civil-rights activists and especially Kennedy's appointment of what Lewis termed "racist judges." Third, the text of Lewis' speech contained inflammatory phrases that could alienate white civil-rights supporters.

Lewis' speech could negatively affect the deliberation on the civil-rights bill. Some influential whites threatened to withdraw from the program if Lewis was permitted to deliver his speech in its original text. Randolph was able to persuade Lewis to modify his speech.

King's "I Have a Dream" speech was the most memorable of all those delivered. It also was less critical of the Kennedy administration than many had anticipated it would be. Its focus was on the unkept promises and the broken dreams experienced by African-Americans, as well as King's vision of the "promised land" of better race relations in the future.

Charles C. Jackson

Mariel Boat Lift

Cuban refugees fill the deck of a shrimp boat as it pulls into harbor at Key West, Florida, in May 1980 at the end of its journey from the port of Mariel in Cuba.

Cubans immigrated in great numbers to the United States after the Cuban Revolution ended in 1959 and their government became communist (SEE Cuban Revolution). In early 1980, several groups of Cubans tried to take refuge at various foreign embassies in Havana in an effort to leave the island. During one of these attempts, a Cuban guard was accidentally killed while preventing a group of Cubans from seeking political asylum at the Peruvian embassy. The incident resulted in friction between the Cuban and Peruvian governments.

On April 4, the Cuban government announced the withdrawal of the military guard around the Peruvian embassy. Within twenty-four hours, 10,800 men, women, and children occupied the embassy in hopes of obtaining political asylum.

For two weeks, millions of television viewers in the United States and other nations became aware of the unsanitary conditions and the lack of food, water, and shelter faced by these people. This created a serious image problem for the Cuban government, prompting Fidel Castro to establish a temporary airlift to Costa Rica. The Cuban refugees caused Castro more embarrassment by chanting "Freedom! Freedom!" as the media recorded their arrival in San José.

In response to this negative publicity, Castro permitted Cubans to leave through the port of Mariel, twenty miles west of Havana. Castro challenged Cuban Americans in Miami to come and pick up their relatives, but when the Cuban Americans arrived in boats and makeshift watercraft, they were forced to return to the United States not with their relatives but with people Castro considered undesirable. These included people with criminal records, homosexuals, patients in mental institutions, people who were unable to hear or speak, and people who had leprosy.

Approximately 26,000 of the 125,000 Mariel refugees had criminal records, but many of them had been jailed for stealing food, trading in the black market, or committing political offenses rather than violent crimes. Only about four percent of the *Marielitos*, as they came to be called, were real criminals.

As a whole, Mariel refugees were perceived as being different from those who had immigrated earlier. They were considered to be from a lower class and to have a different set of values. It took months before studies on the Mariel population disproved these beliefs.

José A. Carmona

CAUSES AND EFFECTS

Cubans stormed the Peruvian embassy in Havana in an attempt to leave their communist-governed country. Media coverage of their plight greatly embarrassed Castro and his government and forced him to react.

Castro opened the port of Mariel, allowing Cubans to escape and join their relatives in the United States. Almost 125,000 Cubans arrived as refugees in the United States in approximately five months.

SEE ALSO:
CUBAN REVOLUTION.

Maryland Act of Religious Toleration

CAUSES AND EFFECTS

Although religious toleration was an important principle in Maryland since its founding, civil war in England, especially the events surrounding the execution of King Charles I in 1649, prompted the colonists to reaffirm the conditions under which they would be governed. The law provided for freedom of conscience for all Christian colonists in Maryland. It was an important step toward the religious freedom guaranteed later in the First Amendment to the U.S. Constitution, passed in 1791.

SEE ALSO:
BRITISH SETTLEMENT;
COLONIAL AMERICA;
FIRST AMENDMENT;
SEPARATION OF
CHURCH & STATE.

Cecilius Calvert, the second Lord Baltimore and the founder of the colony of Maryland, drafted the act of religious toleration that protected Christians from one another.

Although the colony of Maryland was planned mainly as a refuge for Roman Catholics, who were persecuted in their native England, the colony had always accepted and even encouraged settlement by Protestants. In 1633, Catholics and Protestants sailing for the New Land were under strict orders to avoid religious controversy, and they had done so. The two groups got along well, and occasional offenders such as those who were accused of proselytizing or interfering with religious practice were tried and punished.

The political events in England that led to the execution of King Charles I in January 1649 marked a turning point in British history. For the first time, a British monarch had been condemned and executed by the people, acting as a group with the belief that the king's right to rule was limited if he interfered with their liberty. British subjects no longer considered the monarch's right to rule as absolute and God given. In the colonies, this translated to a new way of thinking about the role of government—a way of thinking that spread faster and deeper because the colonies were physically distant from England. Increasingly, the people demanded a voice in establishing the rules under which they would live.

When Cecilius Calvert, the second Lord Baltimore, drafted the charter that created the Maryland colony, he had included the strict toleration of religious differences. When Charles I was killed, Lord Baltimore recognized that the authority given him by the charter would be decreased. He submitted to the colony's General Assembly a series of sixteen laws, including the document "An Act Concerning Religion," also known as the Toleration Act. Not all the proposals were adopted by the assembly, but the Toleration Act was approved on April 21, 1649, establishing by the will of the people that no Christian citizen should be "any waies troubled, molested or discountenanced, for or in respect of his or her Religion." It was the first time in modern history that people had chosen to protect religious freedom.

Cynthia A. Bily

Mayan Civilization

The Mayan civilization developed in the northern part of Central America, southwestern Mexico, and the Yucatán Peninsula perhaps as early as 2500 B.C.E. (SEE Mesoamerican Civilizations). The Classic period, which was between 200 or 250 C.E. and 900 C.E., was a period of dynamic change when Mayan intellectual and artistic achievements reached their height. Although the Maya displayed considerable cultural uniformity, regional differences were significant, especially in art, architecture, and city planning.

The Mayan region can be divided into three parts. The highlands, in western Guatemala, El Salvador, and southeastern Mexico, are made up of two mountain ranges where volcanoes, steep-sided gorges, fertile valleys, and lakes can be found. Directly to the north are the lowlands, a limestone plateau that has an elevation of seven hundred feet (213 meters) or less. It is an area of hills, escarpments, grassy savannas, and seasonal swamps.

Several rivers drain the area, and a series of lakes extend from east to west. Large portions of the southern lowlands are covered with rain forest and are subject to extreme heat, humidity, and very heavy rainfall during the rainy season.

The northern lowlands are farther north on the Yucatán Peninsula and are almost completely flat. The meager rainfall in the area quickly sinks into the porous limestone. The limestone crust has collapsed into the underground drainage system, creating cenotes, or natural wells. Vegetation is the dry-land shrub variety. Despite unfavorable climatic conditions, poor soils, and dense vegetation, it was here that Mayan civilization achieved its highest development.

EARLY AND LATE PRE-CLASSIC PERIODS

The Maya developed settled village life perhaps as early as 2000 B.C.E. As the number and size of the villages increased, the Maya spread into different environmental zones and came into contact with neighboring

A carved pier at the Temple of the Warriors faces the neighboring Kukuklan temple, which lies on the top of a square-based pyramid in Chichén Itzá, the most famous site of an ancient Mayan city in Mexico.

peoples. This period, the early pre-Classic, lasted until about 200 or 300 B.C.E.

The late pre-Classic period, between 200 B.C.E. and 200 C.E., marks the emergence of the cultural features characteristic of Classic Mayan civilization: monumental architecture, hieroglyphic writing, polychrome pottery, and large ceremonial centers. Extensive trade was conducted on land and in the Gulf of Mexico. The dominant cities were located in the highlands and controlled trade in valuable products such as obsidian

SUMMARY

➢ The Mayan civilization developed around 2500 B.C.E.
➢ The late pre-Classic period, from 200 B.C.E. to 200 C.E., marks the emergence of the cultural features characteristic of Classic Mayan civilization: monumental architecture, hieroglyphic writing, polychrome pottery, and large ceremonial centers.
➢ The cause of the Mayan civilization's collapse is unknown, but one theory is that the food supply became inadequate.

A fresco painting depicts a procession of musicians in a decoration on a Mayan tomb in Bonampak, southern Mexico.

DAILY LIFE

MAYAN FAMILY LIFE

The basic unit of Mayan society was the patrilocal family (a family centered around the father's home). Maya families normally lived in simply furnished, one-room houses that sat upon a low platform for drainage and ventilation. Houses were usually built in groups of three or more around a patio.

Women wore long skirts, shawls, and blouselike tops that were sometimes elaborately decorated. Men wore long, sometimes decorated loincloths that hung down in front and back. In cool weather or on special occasions, they wore sleeveless jackets and mantles. Jewelry made of jade, shells, or amber was worn in the earlobe, nostril, septum, or lip by both men and women.

Women prepared the meals, kept the house, raised children, and wove cloth. Men tilled the fields, hunted, served as musicians and craftsmen, and built the houses.

The birth of a child was considered the most significant event in the life of a Maya. Immediately after birth, the child was washed and placed in a cradle with the forehead flattened between two boards. As soon as possible, the parents consulted a priest, who named the child and forecast its destiny. A puberty ceremony was held for girls at age twelve and for boys at fourteen. After the ceremony, girls were considered ready for marriage but continued to live at home until married, usually two to four years later, and boys lived in communal houses.

Boys painted themselves black until marriage, which was arranged by go-betweens. Strict rules governed the selection of marriage partners. After marriage, men and women decorated themselves from the waist up, using tattooing and scarification, and were expected to be monogamous, except for important men, who could take more than one wife. Although adultery was considered a serious offense punishable by death, adultery and sexual promiscuity were widespread.

and cacao. Construction of monumental sculptures and the development of hieroglyphs and calendars began at these sites.

By the end of the late pre-Classic period, the dominance of the highlands was broken, and the center of the economy shifted to the lowlands. The eruption of Ilopango volcano in El Salvador may have adversely affected the highlands environment, causing migration to the lowlands.

THE CLASSIC PERIOD

The Maya traded extensively both south into Central America and north into central Mexico. Most of the goods were transported in large canoes along the coast, and were then carried inland to markets. Salt (an important item of commerce), honey, cotton mantles, and slaves were widely traded. Regional trade items were quetzal feathers, flint and chert, obsidian, colored shells, jade, and cacao, which was used for money as well as chocolate.

The Maya cultivated maize, beans, pumpkins, tomatoes, chili peppers, and root crops such as sweet potatoes, jicama, and yucca. Papayas, avocados, sapodillos, custard apples, and breadfruit were also cultivated, and wild fruit was collected. For meat, they ate quail, wild duck, wild pigeon, partridge, deer, turkey, peccary (a type of wild hog), fish, turtle, and domesticated dog. The staple of the Mayan diet was maize, which was made into *atole*, *posol*, and tamales. *Atole* was a cornmeal gruel eaten with chili peppers as the first meal of the day, and *posol* was a mixture of water and a sour dough carried into the fields in a gourd to be eaten during the day. Stews made with vegetables and meat with squash seeds and peppers completed the diet. The Maya kept bees for honey and wax. Peasants had free time to enjoy ball games, religious festivals, dancing, feasting, drinking, and storytelling.

Illness and misfortune were believed to be caused by evil spirits or the disfavor of the gods. To alleviate illness or misfortune, medicine men used rituals as well as medicines made from herbs, plants, and

A sculpture known as Chac-mool *stands among the ruins at Chichén Itzá.*

CAUSES AND EFFECTS

There is no undisputed, precise explanation for the early rise of Mayan civilization. The Izapan civilization, which occupied the middle ground both spacially and temporally between the Olmecs and the early Classic period Maya, is theorized to be important to the development of the Mayan civilization. The Izapan were located from Veracruz through Chiapas to the Pacific coast of Guatemala and up to the Guatemala City area. The Izapan developed large sites and produced elaborate art.

Through trade, the Maya came into contact with the more highly developed cultures of the Olmecs and Zapotecs of Mexico, who introduced them to art forms, hieroglyphic writing, and calendars. The Maya developed this heritage and spread it from the middle of Mexico to Central America.

743

various animal parts. Death was feared since no one, it was believed, automatically went to paradise. Ordinary people were buried beneath the floors of their houses with items of daily life and food and with a jade bead in the mouth. Nobles and priests were cremated or buried in funerary temples or mausoleums that contained numerous and elaborate burial objects.

A number of trends can be discerned in the Classic period. One of the most significant was an increase in the population throughout the lowlands. Formerly uninhabited areas were settled, and new cities were founded. As the population grew, the cities expanded around their core, indicating that people were engaged in such specialized pursuits as art, public works, administrative

Modern Mayan girls, descendants of the ancient people, wear colorful traditional dress in Atitlán, Guatemala.

duties, and commerce. The population of the centers cannot be accurately estimated, but the lowlands may have had a population that was between one and two million, and Tikal, the area's largest city, a population of forty to fifty thousand.

The upper class increased in power and wealth, and society became more stratified. The middle class increased as a result of commerce and an increase in the number of artisans, but social mobility decreased. A very large gap between the classes developed. The elite had sole responsibility for astronomy, the calendars, rituals, and divination.

Advances that were made in agricultural techniques provided support for a continually increasing population that included more people who were not engaged in producing food. They included terracing, ridging, the reclamation of swamp lands, and more intensive forms of cultivation.

THE DECLINE

By the eighth century, Mayan society was starting to show signs of strain, and the central Mexican city of Teotihuacán and the highland city of Kaminaljuyu, conquered by Teotihuacán, began to exert external pressure, the exact nature of which is not known. At the end of the Classic period, the population may have outgrown the food supply. Competition for land may have led to battles between cities. Captives taken in these battles may have been used for agriculture, urban labor, or sacrifices.

In the late eighth and early ninth centuries, the construction of large-scale buildings and carving of monumental sculptures stopped, the population declined, and the cities were abandoned. Possible explanations for the collapse of the Mayan civilization include natural disasters, epidemics, agricultural failures, and political upheavals, but its real cause remains a mystery. The most probable explanation lies with increased pressure on the food supply caused by the increase in the non-food-producing portion of society. Also attempts to increase agricultural production may have led to environmental disaster. The construction of temples, palaces, and religious monuments required massive amounts of labor, putting a strain on

TEMPER OF THE TIMES

MAYAN MATH

Hieroglyphic writing and calendars may have originated north of the Maya, with the Zapotecs in Oaxaca and with the Olmecs in Veracruz and Tabasco, but these numeric skills were developed extensively by the Maya. The Maya invented a vigesimal (based on twenty) numbering system. Vertical placement indicated value. There were seven levels. The lowest level indicated numbers up to twenty, the next was for the number of 20's, 400's, 8,000's, 160,000's, 3.2 millions, and 64 millions. A stylized shell represented zero, a dot one, and a bar five. Six was a bar with a dot centered over it.

Using this numbering system, the Maya made very accurate astronomical observations and devised a solar calendar of 365 days. The year had eighteen months of twenty days each and five very unlucky days at its end. A second calendar had 260 days. This calendar had two cycles. One cycle had thirteen numbered days, the other had twenty named days, and both ran at the same time. It took 260 days for the first named and the first numbered day to coincide. A calendar round of fifty-two years was required for the first named day, the first numbered day, and the first day of the solar calendar to coincide.

The Maya used hieroglyphic writing to record religious and historical events. Although the Spanish destroyed most of the Mayan writings, the *Popol Vuh* survived. It records the origins of the Mayan gods and the appropriate sacrifices for each of them. It contains the story of the three failed attempts of the gods to create men and women and the fourth, successful one. The *Popol Vuh* describes the relationship between people and the gods and between the gods and the constellations. It also explains how the gods determined the names and characteristics of animals, plants, and trees. Thus, the *Popul Vuh* was the Mayan holy book— the Mayan explanation of the origins of the universe and all that is in it.

the labor supply and possibly reducing the agricultural workforce. The Mayan lowlands did not control any basic resources but traded in goods made by their skilled artisans.

As population decreased and the cities were abandoned, trade declined. The latest evidence indicates that the collapse was not complete. Cities in the southern lowlands ceased to function while other cities thrived. The Classic traditions lived on in the southern and northern highlands.

Robert D. Talbott

The Mayan civilization began in the Yucatán Peninsula in 2500 B.C.E. and developed over the following three-and-a-half thousand years.

SEE ALSO:
AZTEC EMPIRE;
MESOAMERICAN
CIVILIZATIONS; SPANISH
CONQUEST.

FURTHER READING

•Coe, Michael D. *The Maya.* London: Thames and Hudson, 1980.
•Gallenkamp, Charles. *Maya: The Riddle and Rediscovery of a Lost Civilization.* New York: David McKay, 1976.
•Gallenkamp, Charles, and Regina Elise Johnson, eds. *Maya: Treasures of an Ancient Civilization.* New York: Harry N. Abrams, 1985.
•Hammond, Norman. *Ancient Maya Civilization.* New Brunswick, N.J.: Rutgers University Press, 1982.
•_____, ed. *Social Process in Maya Prehistory: Studies Honor of Sir Eric Thompson.* New York: Academic Press, 1977.
•Sabloff, Jeremy A., and E. Wyllys Andrews V. *Late Lowland Maya Civilization: Classic to Postclassic.* Albuquerque: University of New Mexico Press, 1986.
•Tedlock, Dennis, trans. *Popol Vuh: The Definitive Edition of the Maya Book of the Dawn of Life and Glories of Gods and Kings.* New York: Simon & Schuster, 1985.

Medicine Lodge Creek Treaty

SUMMARY

➤ The Sand Creek Massacre (1864) and the Fetterman Massacre (1866) focused attention on the need for an Indian policy.
➤ In 1867, Commissioner of Indian Affairs Nathaniel Taylor was ordered to negotiate peace with the Indians.
➤ In October 1867, the Kiowa, Comanche, Apache, Cheyenne, and Arapaho tribes gathered at Medicine Lodge Creek and signed a peace treaty.
➤ The Indians retained the right to hunt the buffalo and were given thirty-year annuities in return for settlement on reservations.

The Civil War so consumed the American people that U.S. lawmakers had no time to develop an American Indian policy for the U.S. military. Gold miners had begun traveling the Bozeman Trail to the Montana mines in 1864, and Colonel Henry B. Carrington arrived at Fort Laramie in 1866 to build forts along the trail. On December 21, 1866, Red Cloud, High Back Bone, and Crazy Horse, leading a group of Sioux, Cheyenne, and Arapaho, successfully staged an attack on Captain William J. Fetterman and eighty soldiers who had built a guardian stockade at Little Piney Creek (SEE Bozeman Trail War). Every soldier was slain in what has since been called the Fetterman Massacre.

The Fetterman Massacre, coming on the heels of the Sand Creek Massacre in Colorado (November 29, 1864), in which hundreds of Cheyenne were killed, thrust the issue of Indian policy into the spotlight. Peace with the Great Plains Indians was not

U.S. cavalrymen find the remains of Captain Fetterman's column after it was wiped out by Indians in Dakota territory in 1866. In 1867, at Medicine Lodge Creek, the United States signed a peace treaty with the Indians.

every American's goal. Traditionally, the Senate preferred peace and the House war. When Senator James Doolittle, a Republican from Wisconsin, spoke in Denver in July 1865, in the same opera house where the scalps of the Cheyenne murdered at Sand Creek had been displayed, he asked whether the Indians should be placed on reservations or simply exterminated. The capacity crowd cried: "Exterminate them!" Though the Sand Creek Massacre had awakened sympathy for the Indians among Easterners, Westerners appeared increasingly in favor of violence.

Doolittle's report on the state of Indian affairs was published in January 1867, and was used in the debate over whether the

Indian Bureau should remain in the Interior Department or be moved to the War Department. In May 1867, the secretary of the War Department protested that such an action would force the Indians into a war, and the Sully Commission, which had investigated the Fetterman Massacre, reported that all the Indians of the northern Great Plains wanted peace.

Black Kettle, the leading Cheyenne chief at Medicine Lodge Creek and a survivor of the Sand Creek Massacre (SEE Sand Creek Massacre), had signed the Little Arkansas Treaty in 1865, but the Cheyenne Dog Soldiers were not so willing to give up their hunting grounds in western Kansas, and hostilities continued throughout the summer of 1867. However, peace was still favored by most of the Great Plains tribes. In July 1867, a commission headed by Commissioner of Indian Affairs Nathaniel Taylor, was charged with negotiating a peace.

The great treaty council was held in October 1867, in a valley of Medicine Lodge Creek, south of Fort Larned, Kansas. Almost every chief of importance on the southern Great Plains signed the Medicine Lodge Creek Treaty, which the Department of the Interior recorded as three separate treaties: the Treaty Between the United States of America and the Kiowa and Comanche Tribes of Indians, dated October 21, 1867; the Treaty Between the United States of America and the Confederation Kiowa, Comanche, and Apache Tribes, dated October 21, 1867; and the Treaty Between the United States of America and the Arapaho and Cheyenne Tribes, dated October 28, 1867.

The signatures included those of Satank (Sitting Bear), Satanta (White Bear), Black Eagle, Kicking Eagle, Stinking Saddle, Woman's Heart, Stumbling Bear, One Bear, The Crow, and Bear Lying Down of the Kiowa; Ten Bears, Painted Lips, Silver Brooch, Standing Feather, Gap in the Woods, Horse's Back, Wolf's Name, Little Horn, Iron Mountain, and Dog Fat of the

Red Cloud led his Oglala tribe to notable victories over U.S. forces after the Medicine Lodge Creek Treaty was broken.

PROFILE

SATANTA (WHITE BEAR; C. 1830–1878)

Known as the Orator of the Plains, Satanta, or White Bear, spent his life fighting the United States government's efforts to force the Kiowa and Comanche nations onto reservations. One of the Native American leaders who signed the Medicine Lodge Creek Treaty, Satanta nevertheless eloquently predicted the fate he foresaw for the indigenous peoples of the Plains: "I love the land and the buffalo, and will not part with it. . . . I want the children raised as I was. . . . A long time ago this land belonged to our fathers, but when I go up to the river I see camps of soldiers on its banks.

"These soldiers cut down my timber, they kill my buffalo, and when I see that, my heart feels like bursting. . . . This is our country. We have always lived in it. We always had plenty to eat because the land was full of buffalo. We were happy. . . . Then you came. . . . We have to protect ourselves. We have to save our country. We have to fight for what is ours."

FURTHER READING

•Armstrong, Virginia, ed. *I Have Spoken: American History Through the Voices of the Indians.* New York: Pocket Books, 1972.

•Berthrong, Donald J. *The Cheyenne and Arapahoe Ordeal: Reservation and Agency Life in the Indian Territory, 1875–1907.* Norman: University of Oklahoma Press, 1976.

•Jones, Douglas C. *The Treaty of Medicine Lodge.* Norman: University of Oklahoma Press, 1966.

•Josephy, Alvin M., Jr. *Five Hundred Nations: An Illustrated History of North American Indians.* New York: Alfred A. Knopf, 1994.

CAUSES AND EFFECTS

Consolidating the Indians north of the Platte River and south of the Arkansas River would open territory between the rivers and make it possible to complete the Union Pacific and Kansas Pacific Railroads. The Medicine Lodge Creek Treaty (1867) helped open the land, but peace was gone from the plains by summer 1868. The first annuity issue under the treaty did not include the promised weapons, so a party of young Cheyenne raided Kansas settlements. Major G. A. Forsyth and plainsmen acting as scouts went after the Cheyenne war party only to be surrounded and nearly wiped out in the incident known as Beecher's Island. In November Lieutenant Colonel George Custer countered by attacking Black Kettle's peaceful Cheyenne village on the Washita River, killing Black Kettle and many others.

Comanche; Black Kettle, Tall Bull, Little Robe, and Bull Bear of the Cheyenne; Wolf's Sleeve, Poor Bear, Bad Back, Brave Man, Iron Shirt, and White Horn of the Apaches; and Little Raven of the Arapaho. The treaty terms established annuities for thirty years and the right to hunt the buffalo as long as the buffalo ran. In return, the Indian people accepted settlement on reservations and education in schools to assimilate them into the Euro-American lifestyle. Reservation lands were those that had been taken from the Five Civilized Tribes as part of their punishment for siding with the South in the Civil War (SEE Southeastern American Indians). Article I of the Medicine Lodge Creek Treaty stated: "From this day forward all war between the parties to this agreement shall forever cease." The Fort Laramie Treaty of 1868 was also intended to create peace, but the inability of the U.S. government to fulfill its obligations

of supplying food and materials, the relocation and removal of Indian peoples, and the railroad expansion and increasing westward movement of white settlers combined with other factors to destroy the commitment to peace (SEE Westward Expansion).

By October 1868, the treaty seemed dead. The Great Plains Indians and the U.S. military countered each other's actions. Lieutenant Colonel George Custer's dawn attack on Black Kettle's sleeping Cheyenne village on the Washita River, November 27, 1868, resulted in the massacre of a people who believed they were protected by treaties promising peace (SEE Washita River Massacre). Black Kettle, eternal champion of peace, was murdered in the attack.

Tonya Huber

The meeting at Fort Laramie, Wyoming, in 1868, when a treaty was signed that created the Great Sioux Reservation.

Meighen's Ministry

Arthur Meighen (1874–1960) became the ninth Canadian prime minister on July 10, 1920, when he succeeded Robert Borden, who had served as prime minister from 1911 to 1920. During World War I, Meighen had served as minister of justice. The Conservative Party member was anything but tactful in dealing with political opponents. When fellow members of Parliament from Quebec expressed opposition to military conscription because of their belief that purely Canadian interests were not involved, he referred to Quebecers as "a backward people." He also offended Canadians of Austrian and German descent by proposing a law that stripped such Canadians, who had become citizens after 1902, of the right to vote. Quebecers and ethnic Canadians never forgave Meighen for questioning their intelligence and patriotism.

Meighen served twice as the prime minister of Canada, first from July 1920 to December 1921 and then for three days in the summer of 1926. During World War I, he had argued that it was Britain's right to determine Canada's foreign policy, but in June 1921 he stated that henceforth Canada would not accept British control over Canadian foreign policy. He seemed inconsistent. His chances for victory in the December 1921 election became slimmer because Canadian voters blamed him for the economic downturn of 1920 and 1921. The Liberals under William Lyon Mackenzie King easily won the election.

Neither the Liberals nor the Conservatives, however, won a majority in the October 1925 general election. King formed a coalition with minor parties, but he then asked Lord Julian Byng, governor-general of Canada, to dissolve Parliament. Lord Byng refused and asked Meighen to form a new government. King argued that Byng's action constituted a violation of Canadian independence and called for a vote of no confidence. Meighen lost by one vote. His second term as prime minister lasted just three days.

The Liberals won an absolute majority in the September 1926 general election.

Arthur Meighen became the Canadian prime minister during the difficult postwar years following World War I.

CAUSES AND EFFECTS

Although Arthur Meighen was a very honest politician, his lack of tact and insensitivity to the feelings of Quebecers and ethnic minorities made it almost impossible for him to win general elections in Canada. Choosing Meighen to succeed Robert Borden proved to be a disaster for the Conservative Party because it persuaded Quebecers and ethnic Canadians that the Conservatives did not care about them. Between 1921 and 1957, the Conservatives won only the election of 1930.

Meighen's political influence had ended. He became an investment banker in Toronto and died in 1960.

Edmund J. Campion

SEE ALSO:
BORDEN'S MINISTRY;
KING'S MINISTRIES.

Mercantilism

SUMMARY

➤ Mercantilism, which was practiced by Western European countries in the sixteenth and seventeenth centuries, held that a nation's ability to accumulate wealth demonstrated its economic and political strength.

➤ This belief, which included the desire to obtain raw goods as cheaply as possible to maximize the profit on manufactured products, led to England, France, and Spain acquiring and developing colonies.

➤ England, France, and Spain placed strict restrictions on colonial trade in an attempt to maintain tight control.

➤ A large part of the wealth generated by trade with colonies was spent on protecting them and battling with economic rivals.

Mercantilism, an economic concept, was practiced by the countries of Western Europe during the sixteenth and seventeenth centuries. The newly developing nation-states of the continent—England, France, Spain, Portugal, and the Netherlands—had begun to compete with one another, seeking to achieve economic advantage. Though the term was not adopted until two centuries later, the basic concept of mercantilism held that a nation's ability to accumulate wealth demonstrated its economic and political strength. The proponents of mercantilism reasoned that increasing a country's treasury through the acquisition of gold and silver added to its power relative to that of its political and economic rivals.

Between 1550 and 1700, Western Europe underwent a series of major political changes. Power became increasingly centralized as strong monarchies arose to replace the fragmented feudal political systems of the Middle Ages. This central control led to systematized taxation, standard coinage, and

King Louis XIV of France (seated) strongly encouraged mercantilism, whereby European nations developed colonies to gather wealth.

improved communication and methods of land and sea transportation. Having achieved this centralization of power, the rulers sought to develop a comprehensive economic and political plan for their respective countries.

The search for increased economic and political strength led the Western European countries to undertake a massive program of exploration. Spain, Portugal, England, France, and the Netherlands began to send well-organized expeditions to Africa, Asia, and the Western Hemisphere in hopes of opening trade routes that would aid in their economic development. The Western European rulers adopted a plan of selling monopolies to certain of their citizens to encourage the exploitation of the newly discovered territories. This technique guaranteed the Crown a certain percentage of the wealth extracted by the entrepreneurs and relieved it of the burden of funding the expeditions. The rulers often imposed tariffs to protect home industry and to discourage the export of goods considered vital to the country's productive capacity.

Competition for overseas wealth and resources led to the establishment of and struggle for permanent colonies. According to a basic tenet of mercantilism, to achieve a favorable balance of trade the raw materials necessary for manufacturing had to be acquired at the lowest cost possible to maximize the profit on finished goods exported for sale.

If a country had limited natural resources, the acquisition of overseas colonies to furnish these resources became critical in the mercantilist equation. The state could dictate to its colonial possession the type and price of raw material sought from the colony for manufacturing at home. The colony could also be used as a market for the finished goods produced by the mother country.

The scramble for colonies during the sixteenth and seventeenth centuries led to competition among the European powers and ultimately to an almost continuous series of wars, both at home and overseas. To protect their newly acquired possessions and the trade routes that led to them, nations required expensive standing armies, formidable navies, and the construction of immense fortifications to protect key seaports. Much of the wealth that was accumulated under mercantilism was spent on armaments required to maintain both military personnel and installations.

The three major colonial powers operating in North America were England, France, and Spain, although the Dutch also played a small role in this area. All of those nations endeavored to establish economic and political systems designed to ensure a competitive advantage. Continued warfare among the three rivals proved to be the rule rather than the exception.

ENGLAND AND MERCANTILISM

England's Parliament passed the Navigation Ordinances of 1650 and 1651, which mandated that all goods entering English ports must be carried on ships built, owned, and manned by English subjects. Exports were governed by the same regulations. The restrictions were aimed at encouraging the development of England's maritime capabilities and adding to its favorable balance of trade. Of all the trading nations competing in the sixteenth century, England perhaps enjoyed the greatest success in terms of raising the standard of living of its citizens. Unlike its rivals, France and Spain, England allowed its middle-class tradesmen and manufacturers to participate to some degree in the profits from the overseas bonanza.

The English crown's mercantilist economic policies concerning its North American colonies proved to be counterproductive in the long run. During the eighteenth century, Taxation Without Representation became the rallying cry of

The shipbuilders of Europe were kept extremely busy during the age of mercantilism. Well-built, modern ships were required to exploit the resources of lands across the seas.

CAUSES AND EFFECTS

The economic concept of mercantilism arose as a result of the development in the seventeenth century of strong, centralized nation-states in Western Europe. The new national rulers devised economic programs designed to consolidate and perpetuate their power. The key to mercantilist thinking lay in developing a favorable balance of trade with foreign countries. The trade surplus would be held in gold and silver, which the mercantilists believed would ensure the economic and political well-being of the home country. Colonies existed for the economic benefit of their discoverers, to provide raw materials for conversion to finished goods at home. The mother country, in turn, would sell the finished product back to the colonies at a profit.

In practice, mercantilism created intense competition and rivalry among its advocates. Relationships among its leading practitioners became increasingly warlike, and much of the wealth arising from commerce had to be diverted to the maintenance of standing armies and navies. The substantial influx of silver and gold into the European continent through Spain created inflationary pressures on local economies as well.

All the proponents of mercantilism could not, however, achieve the desired favorable balance of trade. Under mercantilism, all participants could not be winners; somebody had to lose. The extreme protectionism adopted by the leading commercial countries could lead only to a restriction of trade rather than to its expansion. Moreover, the arbitrary decisions of the mother countries concerning their colonies in the Western Hemisphere inevitably led to wars of independence on the part of the colonies in the eighteenth and nineteenth centuries.

the residents of the thirteen colonies on the Atlantic seaboard. The American Revolution that followed cost Britain a substantial portion of its possessions.

FRANCE, SPAIN, AND MERCANTILISM

France engaged in a series of costly wars with its neighbors in search of a competitive advantage. France's central government, an absolute monarchy, dictated and closely controlled the nation's economic policies. The Crown set regulations for the type of agriculture, industry, and land-and-sea commerce that its subjects could undertake.

Jean-Baptiste Colbert (1619–1683), who served as prime minister for many years, said: "It is only the abundance of money in a state that determines its powers." Recognizing the king and his court's insatiable demand for riches, Colbert urged the monarch to expand French overseas investment in both Canada and its sugar-producing island colonies in the Caribbean. The crown also sought to transfer "loyal French Catholics" to the Western Hemisphere as settlers to give France a firmer grip on its colonial possessions.

Jean-Baptiste Colbert, a French statesman who, during the seventeenth century, masterminded French acquisition of territories in North America and elsewhere.

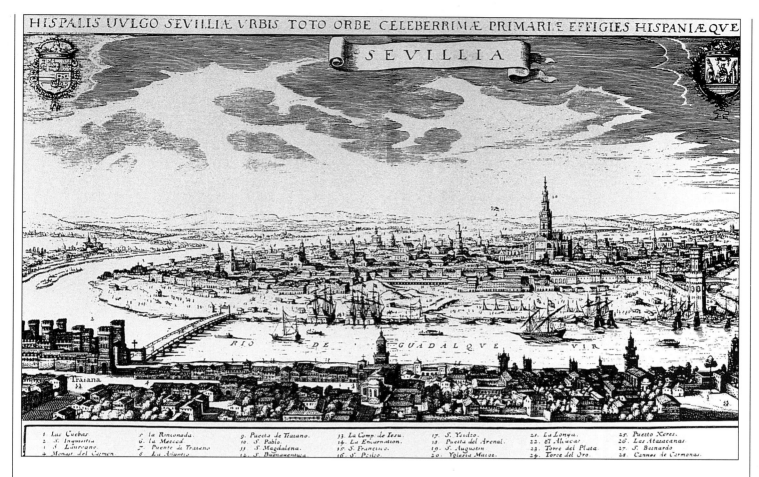

HISPALIS UVLGO SEVILLIÆ VRBIS TOTO ORBE CELEBERRIMÆ PRIMARIÆ EFFIGIES HISPANIÆQVE

SEVILLIA

RIO DE GUADALQVVIR

Traiana

1. Las Cuebas.	5. la Rinconada.	9. Pucrta de Traiano.	13. La Comp. de Iesu.	17. S. Yxidro.	21. La Lonya.	25. Puerto Xeres.
2. S. Inquisitia	6. la Merced	10. S. Pablo.	14. La Encurnation.	18. Pucrta del Arenal.	22. El Alcucar	26. Las Atazacanas
3. S. Laurcano	7. Puente de Traiano	11. S. Magdalena.	15. S. Francisco.	19. S. Augustin	23. Torre del Plata	27. S. Bernardo.
4. Monast. del Carmen.	8. La Asiunito	12. S. Buenaventura.	16. S. Pedro.	20. Yglesia Maior.	24. Torre del Oro.	28. Cannos de Carmonas.

Much of the profit derived from France's overseas trade, however, was wasted by the extravagances of the French monarch and his court. Ordinary French citizens benefited little from the wealth created from overseas trade. Royalty's excesses ultimately led to the French Revolution toward the end of the following century.

The Spanish crown adopted the most restrictive regulations on colonial trade of all the Western European countries. All goods destined to enter its colonies had to pass through Cadiz or Seville, Spain's principal seaports. Also, all goods produced in its colonies had to be shipped to Spain first.

The colonies were forbidden to trade with other European nations or even with each other. Certain goods were prohibited from being produced in the colonies even if they were needed locally. Wine, for example, necessary for religious rituals, could not be manufactured locally but had to be imported from Spain.

Spain, in the long run, could not maintain the control over its sea-lanes or colonies necessary to practice successfully the mercantilist concept of tight control. The country's overseas possessions were too numerous and too widespread to be adequately protected from attacks and incursions by Spain's economic and political competitors. The home economy could not absorb all of the produce of its colonies.

As time went on, the colonies began to smuggle goods and surreptitiously trade with each other and foreign nations rather than remain dependent on the expensive and often tardy delivery of necessities from the mother country. When the Spanish crown encountered problems with the French at home at the beginning of the nineteenth century, the seed was sown for moves toward independence by most of its Western Hemisphere possessions.

The overall effect of the mercantilist system led initially to a dramatic increase in trade between the Western European nations and their colonies in North America as these countries poured a large part of their national wealth into the expansion of the commercial trade potential of the colonies. All the countries involved engaged in a frantic effort

Seville in southern Spain was one of the most important European ports for developing trade with the New World. Shortly after setting sail from Seville, a ship would be on the Atlantic Ocean.

FURTHER READING

•Andrews, Charles M. *The Colonial Period.* Vol. 4, *England's Commercial and Colonial Policy.* New Haven, Conn.: Yale University Press, 1938.

•Cole, Charles W. *Colbert and a Century of French Mercantilism.* Hamden, Conn.: Archon Books, 1964.

•Davis, Ralph. *The Rise of the English Shipping Industry in the Seventeenth and Eighteenth Centuries.* London: David & Charles, 1962.

(Continued on page 754)

FURTHER READING
•Ekelund, Robert B., and Robert D. Tollison. *Mercantilism as a Rent-Seeking Society: Economic Regulation in Historical Perspective.* College Station: Texas A&M University Press, 1981.
•McAlister, Lyle N. *Spain and Portugal in the New World.* Minneapolis: University of Minnesota Press, 1984.
•Magnusson, Lars. *Mercantilism: The Shaping of an Economic Language.* London: Routledge, 1994.
•____, ed. *Mercantilist Economics.* Boston: Kluwer Academic Publishers, 1993.
•Wallbank, T. Walter, and Alastair M. Taylor. *Civilization: Past and Present.* Vol. 2. New York: Scott, Foresman, 1942.

DAILY LIFE

SPANISH GALLEONS

The need to protect its sea-lanes to its distant colonies and to move greater quantities of cargo led the Spanish shipbuilders to develop the galleon in the mid-sixteenth century. These square-rigged, three-masted ships were larger and longer and could carry more cargo than those previously used by the Spaniards.

They were truly floating fortresses, sometimes three and four decks high, armed with wooden castles perched fore and aft and a large compliment of heavy broadside cannon to deter any attacks by pirates in peacetime or enemy ships during war. Galleons served a dual purpose, acting both as men-of-war and as cargo carriers.

The Spanish crown devised a plan to organize two flotillas annually from Spain to the Indies and back, counting on the heavily armed galleons to protect the smaller cargo vessels that accompanied them. Spain set up a trade route between Mexico's west coast at Acapulco and Manila in the Philippines in the same manner. Because much of the inbound cargo from the colonies to Spain consisted of gold and silver and other cargos of high value, ships sailing alone represented an attractive target. As the seventeenth century wore on, the Spanish crown dropped the plan for annual flotillas but continued to advocate a policy of requiring Spanish ships to sail in concert rather than operating alone.

A Spanish treasure fleet of the 1600's assembles at Havana, ready to sail in convoy to Spain.

to produce the necessary ships to carry the cargo that resulted from the trade expansion. Cannon manufacturers and other weapon producers earned immense profits. The demand for ship's officers and sailors also rose precipitously.

In effect, the home countries expended much of the profit derived from this expansion of trade on the manpower and war materials needed to protect the newly acquired wealth from economic and political competitors. By the eighteenth century, most of the European economic powers had chosen broader and more rewarding approaches to economic endeavor. To many, the establishment of peaceful relations with their neighbors through the signing of treaties guaranteeing reciprocal trade provided an effective alternative to the problems created by mercantilism's negative characteristics.

Carl Henry Marcoux

Mesoamerican Civilizations

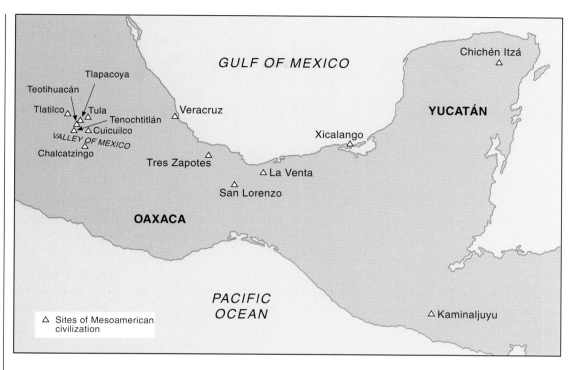

Mesoamerica extended from the mid-north of Mexico into Central America. It was inhabited by a number of highly developed peoples such as the Olmec who developed the cities of Veracruz and La Venta on the coast, Kaminaljuyu to the south, and several centers in the Valley of Mexico. The Maya developed farther south, in the Yucatán Peninsula.

When the first Europeans reached the Americas in the late fifteenth century, they encountered New World civilizations unlike any in the Old World. The first explorers set foot upon the shores of an ancient world of indigenous civilizations whose complexity matched and often surpassed that of cultures in Europe and the Mediterranean.

Mesoamerica, which includes much of present-day Mexico, Guatemala, Belize, Honduras, El Salvador, and Nicaragua, is one of five major world areas that saw the independent origins of state-level civilization and the first formal writing systems. Over thousands of years, Mesoamerica saw the origin and development of many extraordinary civilizations, including the Olmec, Mayan, Teotihuacán, Zapotec, Toltec, Mixtec, and Aztec civilizations.

ORIGINS

Evidence indicates that early peoples settled the margins of lakes in the Valley of Mexico 22,000 years ago. These people were hunters and gatherers who subsisted on available plant and animal resources. Global climatic changes that transformed Mesoamerica 12,000 years ago dramatically altered the world of these early humans and set the stage for rapid cultural changes.

Early farmers cultivated maize and many other plants, including beans, squash, chili, bottle gourd, sweet potatoes, manioc, tomatoes, avocados, cacao, vanilla, rubber, chicle, and tobacco. The primary Mesoamerican food items were corn, beans, and squash, all of which were domesticated more than five thousand years ago.

Successful agriculture promoted settled lifestyles. As populations expanded, vast areas became linked by trade. The demand for resources ranging from cacao and jade to volcanic glass and basalt promoted the growth of towns and cities. Mesoamerica saw the emergence of the monumental civic-ceremonial precincts and plaza-oriented courts and platform mounds, and the adoption of the sacred ball game, a pattern that defined traditions that persisted for the next three thousand years.

OLMEC CIVILIZATION

By 1500 B.C.E., coastal trade resulted in the spread of Olmec, or Gulf Coast, art and culture into other regions of Mesoamerica. The Olmec, whose principal centers were La Venta, Tres Zapotes, San Lorenzo, and

SUMMARY

➤ Mesoamerica is one of five major world areas where state-level civilization and formal writing systems developed.
➤ An early center of civilization was the Olmec village of Cuicuilco, which commanded culture and commerce in the Valley of Mexico until its destruction in 100 B.C.E.
➤ Teotihuacán, which had a monopoly on obsidian, developed a vast trading network and culture that spread through most of Mesoamerica before the city was destroyed in 650 C.E.
➤ The Toltecs, who rose to power through military might, controlled the area from 900 to 1175 C.E.
➤ The Toltecs' rituals were dominated by human sacrifice and combat sports.

CAUSES AND EFFECTS

The global climate changed at the end of the Ice Age, bringing changes upon the plant and animal communities that supported early Mesoamerican hunters. As Mesoamerica grew increasingly warm and dry, areas formerly dominated by vast forests were reduced to semi-arid grasslands, and gigantic Ice Age creatures such as the mammoth and mastodon gradually became extinct.

Early Mesoamerican hunters were forced to adapt to an environment that no longer had an abundance of large game animals nor familiar Ice Age plants. Their diet of mammoth flesh and wild seeds gave way to one of aquatic fowl, shellfish, rabbits, reptiles, rodents, and a variety of grasses and other plants. The eventual domestication and control of such foods allowed early humans to settle into ever larger and more stable communities. Ultimately, these changes opened the door to the invention of agriculture and the domestication of both plants and animals.

The Avenue of the Dead in Teotihuacán, which was the religious center of the Olmec civilization. A powerful religious elite ruled over the Olmec people from Teotihuacán.

Veracruz, were a people whose monumental architecture and sculpture influenced the nature and direction of Mesoamerican society for centuries.

Chalcatzingo was one of the earliest Olmec outposts in highland Mesoamerica. Between 800 and 300 B.C.E., the town dominated highland trade. The exchange of jade and obsidian fueled a period of intense interaction between the highland and coastal peoples. By 900 B.C.E., the Olmec influence was apparent in such early towns and villages as Tlatilco and Tlapacoya, in Mexico; Kaminaljuyu, Guatemala; and Cerros, Belize.

Early Gulf coast interaction with the Valley of Mexico fueled three centuries of prosperity at the ancient center of Cuicuilco. The town was marked by Olmec-inspired craftsmanship in the form of religious icons, monumental architecture, ceramics, and jade and basalt sculpture.

THE CLASSIC ERA

In 100 B.C.E., Cuicuilco was destroyed by a volcanic eruption. The coastal influence was waning, and the rapid growth of the marketplace at Teotihuacán, which was located near the present-day Mexico City, signaled the beginning of a civilization that would dominate Mesoamerican commerce for the next ten centuries.

By 100 B.C.E., Teotihuacán had initiated an ambitious program centered on the construction of a massive civic-ceremonial precinct. Its Avenue of the Dead became the new center of power in highland Mesoamerica. The Pyramids of the Sun, Moon, and Feathered Serpent dominated the

civic and ceremonial landscapes of the Valley of Mexico for seven centuries.

By 500 C.E., Teotihuacán had between 150,000 and 200,000 residents. Constructed on a massive grid, the ancient city's many apartments and temple precincts embodied an austere and institutionalized architectural style. Teotihuacán linked towns and cities as distant as the Maya lowlands eight hundred miles away and kingdoms such as the ancient Zapotec of Oaxaca. The city came to culturally dominate most of Mesoamerica.

Teotihuacán's monopoly in obsidian proved critical to its growth. Obsidian, or volcanic glass, produces a very sharp edge and therefore was a highly desired resource for toolmaking. As much as a fourth of Teotihuacán's craftspeople were employed in the production of obsidian blade tools and related objects.

In time, Teotihuacán faltered under the weight of so extensive a commercial empire. By 550 C.E., the military had gained prominence. By 650 C.E., Teotihuacán was reduced to a smoldering ruin after a cataclysm borne of internal revolt or foreign invasions by any one or more of the new and powerful kingdoms that controlled highland trade.

THE POST-CLASSIC ERA

After Teotihuacán collapsed, the Toltecs of Tula rebuilt highland commerce. From 900 to 1175 C.E., the Toltecs controlled a sizable trade based on obsidian and ceramics. The Toltecs rose to power through military conquest and the control of resources, and therefore, their rituals were dominated by human sacrifice and combat sports. The period between the collapse of Teotihuacán and the emergence of the Aztecs in 1275 C.E. was an age of chaos and bloodshed dominated by warlords.

Life in ancient Tula, as it had been in Teotihuacán, was centered on merchants, craftspeople, and soldiers, who lived within walled and courtyard-oriented compounds of masonry and mud-brick construction. Finely polished ceramics, slender black obsidian blades, hand-forged gold and copper ornaments, and detailed turquoise mosaics were among the hallmarks of the Toltec artistic tradition.

Atop the acropolis of Tula, the Toltec constructed several major platform mounds upon which were situated administrative and religious buildings with sculpted stone and mortar panels depicting flaming and feathered serpents, and eagles and jaguars devouring cactus fruit and human hearts.

Atop the massive platform mound known as the House of Dawn, Toltec craftspeople sculpted two massive feathered-serpent columns and four enormous warriors standing at attention and brandishing dart throwers. The lords and supernaturals of earth, sky, dawn, and death were depicted on various platforms. At several locations within the sacred precinct of ancient Tula, there are massive I-shaped ball courts with banked walls and stone hoops where soldiers played combatlike ball games.

As a result of their wide-ranging conquests and commercial contacts, the Toltec fueled the development of a style of art, architecture, and tradition that spread

Toltec images of giant warriors carved from stone stand on top of a pyramid at Tula, in the Valley of Mexico. The Toltec were a warlike, militaristic people.

DAILY LIFE

LIFE IN TEOTIHUACÁN

The congestion created by the existence of more than two thousand urban apartment compounds placed a premium on the control of urban waste, pollution, and disease in Teotihuacán. The residents constructed a waste-management and water system of subfloor conduits and stone and ceramic pipelines. Many elaborately painted wall murals depicting gods and daily life within the city enhanced and brightened the otherwise austere architectural styles of the ancient center. Clouds of burning incense and the smoke, dust, and congestion of the marketplace were typical of the activity at the heart of Teotihuacán. Foreign merchants and religious pilgrims undoubtedly colored daily life in the otherwise congested metropolis.

The head of Quetzalcoatl, a god that took the form of a plumed serpent, forms a fearsome stone carving created at Teotihuacán.

deep into the heartland and frontiers of Mesoamerica. Tula commanded highland resources and their exchange with ports as distant as Xicalango on the southern Mexican Gulf Coast and Chichén Itzá in the Maya heartland of Mexico's Yucatán peninsula. At Chichén Itzá, Toltec influence is apparent in everything from wall murals and bas-relief panels to sculpted monuments and civic-ceremonial architecture. The House of Dawn is often compared with the Temple of the Warriors at Chichén Itzá. These monuments are so similar that their architectural layout and sculptural plan would not appear out of place in either ancient city. Despite their power, neither Tula nor Chichén Itzá survived the onslaught of the new warrior kings that dominated the thirteenth century.

By 1250 C.E., both cities had faded into memory and their collapse was followed by invasions by the warring tribes of the frontiers of Mesoamerica. During the two centuries before Spanish conqueror Hernán Cortés arrived, the Aztec empire dominated the political scene and cultural landscape of Mesoamerica (SEE Aztec Empire).

Ruben G. Mendoza and Brenda Pobre

DAILY LIFE

THE MESOAMERICAN BALL GAME

Mesoamerican ball-court games originated in the pre-Classic period at approximately 1200 B.C.E. Unlike sports in ancient Egypt, China, Greece, and Rome, the Mesoamerican ball game of the Aztec era was oriented not to individual effort but to collective, combatlike sport and religion-related ceremonial sacrifice and bloodletting. Many versions of the Mesoamerican ball game are known, and more than fifteen types of ball courts have been identified.

What is known of the ball game is derived from historical records from the time of the Spanish conquest and recent interpretations of Mayan glyphs and art. The Aztec and Mayan versions of this sport were played within an I-shaped masonry court with stone ball-court markers set at regular intervals within the floor or on court embankments. In some versions of the game, a vertically positioned stone hoop was set high on a sidewall. Players used a solid rubber ball, cotton-padded leather belts, knee pads, and headgear, and the object of the game was to propel the ball through a stone hoop or past the opposing team's ball-court markers and into their heavily defended court. Known as *ullamalitzli* or *tlatchtli* in the Aztec language and as *pok-ta-pok* in Maya, the Aztec and Mayan versions of the ball game were considered the sport of kings. Sometimes captive rulers and soldiers competed against the very best ballplayers and soldiers of the town or city sponsoring the event. Players propelled a solid rubber ball through the air only by batting it with their hips, knees, shoulders, or arms. It was against the rules to handle, toss, or bat the ball with the hands. After the game, one or more players might be killed in sacrifice.

Many major Mesoamerican cultures, including the Olmec, Mayan, Huastec, Totonac, Zapotec, Toltec, and Aztec, played a version of the ball game. Probably, however, the two greatest of all Mesoamerican ball courts are the ones at Chichén Itzá, with its massive 545-foot-long, 223-foot-wide (166-meter-long, 68-meter-wide) masonry court, and the truly spectacular principal ball court of Aztec Tenochtitlán, which was described by the Spanish who chanced to view the game just before conquering that ancient city.

SEE ALSO:
AZTEC EMPIRE; MAYAN CIVILIZATION; SPANISH CONQUEST.

FURTHER READING
•Blanton, Richard E. "The Emergence of Civilization in Mesoamerica: 1500 B.C.–A.D. 1521." In *New World and Pacific Civilizations: Cultures of America, Asia, and the Pacific*. Vol 4. in *The Illustrated History of Humankind*. San Francisco: HarperCollins, 1994.
•Coe, Michael D. "Early Hunters." In *Mexico*. New York: Praeger, 1971.
•Diehl, Richard A. *Tula: The Toltec Capital of Ancient Mexico*. London: Thames and Hudson, 1983.
•Hunter, C. Bruce. *A Guide to Ancient Mexican Ruins*. Norman: University of Oklahoma Press, 1977.
•Miller, Mary Ellen. *The Art of Mesoamerica from Olmec to Aztec*. New York: Thames and Hudson, 1986.
•Miller, Mary, and Karl Taube. *The Gods and Symbols of Ancient Mexico and the Maya: An Illustrated Dictionary of Mesoamerican Religion*. New York: Thames and Hudson, 1993.
•Weaver, Muriel Porter. *The Aztecs, Maya, and Their Predecessors: Archaeology of Mesoamerica*. 3d ed. San Diego: Academic Press, 1993.

Aztecs playing the combative ball game of tlatchtli at Chichén Itzá.

Mestizos, Metis, & Mulattoes

SUMMARY

➤ Because race is the product of inbreeding, only a few groups, those isolated from contact with other peoples for a long time, can be considered to be close to being racially "pure."
➤ Historically, the intermixing of races has produced great achievements and cultures.
➤ In North America, the races have intermingled, creating mestizos, mulattoes, and Metis.
➤ In the United States, almost as soon as the races intertwined, antimiscegenation legislation arose.
➤ In Mexico, early legislation specifically allowed interracial marriage, and by 1822 the races of the marrying couple were no longer recorded in parish registers.

The mixing of races, or miscegenation, has been a major force in North American social history. Race is a product of inbreeding. Marriage within the group, over generations, spreads any diversity that is created by the influx of a new group of people over the entire population, and the blended characteristics become that group's new racial characteristics.

The only people who are of even relative racial "purity" are those who are part of a group that has long been isolated from contact with other peoples. Eskimos, Southwest desert Indians, some tribes from the interior of Australia, Indamine islanders, and some peoples in the mountains of India are among the groups that come closest to being of pure racial stock. Their purity is the result of their isolation.

The skeletal remains and the artworks of early humans show that the crossing of racial strains was occurring at least as early as the

Two mestizo women stand alongside a white wall in modern Colombia. Mestizos, people of mixed race, make up a significant part of the population of Latin America and Mexico.

beginning of human habitation of the European continent.

Such intermixing occurred wherever one human population met another. In many Latin American countries, for example, mixed-blood groups make up large and important segments of the population. Interracial groups can also be found in most of the port cities of Asia. In India, for example, first the early Portuguese traders and then the British during their occupation of the country intermixed with the locals.

EARLY COLONIAL POLICIES

In Mexico, interracial marriage was explicitly permitted by the Spanish monarch in 1514. The royal decree stated that the lack of

Spanish women made it necessary for Spanish men to marry local Indian women. Two years later, however, colonial authorities were instructed to amend the decree to describe Indian women as "people far from possessing reason."

Throughout colonial times in North America, Indians and African slaves were forced to serve as concubines for the colonizers. The union of European settlers and Indians produced the mestizo, and the union of Europeans with African slaves produced the mulattoes.

The mixture of African slaves and Indians created a population called the zambos, and the metis resulted from the mixture of Indians and European fur traders in Canada. These interminglings created six distinct racial elements in the North American population, each with a rather clearly defined social status in the community.

As interracial people mixed with others, the lines of demarcation became less distinct for some groups. Still, however, the social elite was of largely undiluted European descent. In certain regions of North America, especially areas populated largely by northern European immigrants, a rather

sharp color line began to separate the whites from the non-whites. Usually the line placed the blacks and Indians on one side and the whites and metis on the other. The mixed-blood groups bridged the gap between the country's racial and cultural extremes.

In the United States, the intermixture of blacks and whites seems to have begun almost as soon as African slaves became part of the colonial population, and the opposition to their mingling seems to have arisen almost simultaneously.

The first legislation created was in the colony of Maryland. In 1661, questions first arose as to the status of white servants and the children they bore with black slaves. In 1681, the colony created a supplementary act stipulating that any freeborn woman married to a slave by permission of the slave's master should be free and her children should also be free. It further provided that the slave's master or mistress and the person performing the marriage ceremony should be penalized by fine. In 1715 and 1717, the penalties were made more severe.

Under the new legislation, any white man or woman who cohabited with an African-American would be forced into servitude for

CAUSES AND EFFECTS

The inevitable result of migration, voluntary or forced, in a populated world is contact between races and cultures and their eventual mixture. In the North American colonial societies, colonizers imposed themselves on slaves and native peoples and forcefully brought about the mixture of races.

The Civil Rights movement was a vast effort at integration and a result of opposition to prejudice. Later, American blacks embraced blackness and their roots in Africa, identifying themselves as African-Americans. One of the results of this type of thinking, multiculturalism, placed the emphasis on tolerance and acceptance of cultural and ethnic diversity, providing a background for racial respect.

A Brazilian mulatto soldier presents arms in this seventeenth century image.

seven years. The children created from such a union were to be servants for thirty-one years. The African-American spouse, if free, would become a slave for the rest of that individual's life.

In the Act of 1893, Arizona forbade marriage between whites and Native Americans, Asian-Americans, and African-Americans as well as their descendants. Any existing interracial marriages were declared null and void.

Other states with similar laws included Arkansas, California, Colorado, Delaware, Florida, Georgia, Idaho, Indiana, Louisiana, and Kentucky. The laws of South Dakota, Oregon, Utah, and South Carolina went further; they prohibited marriages between

whites and any Native American, African-American, Korean-American, Malayan, or Asian-American. The penalty was a fine not exceeding $1,000, imprisonment not exceeding ten years, or both.

In other parts of North America, political emancipation tangibly affected the perception of people of mixed race. In Mexico, although mestizos and mulattoes were preferred as house and personal servants during the slavery period, they were subjected to the same kinds of abuses as were African and Indian slaves. Sometimes, the master of the house or plantation forced women slaves to bear offspring to add to the slave population.

In November 1810, José María Morelos y Pavón, a priest who was first the principal aide of and later successor to Miguel Hidalgo y Costilla (a leader during the Mexican Revolution), and a mestizo himself, prohibited the use of labels such as Indian, mulattoes, and *casta*, or caste. Moreover, by 1822 it was no longer necessary to specify ethnicity in parish marriage registers; everybody was termed Mexican.

The decree of 1812 also opened the doors of universities, seminaries, and the priesthood to mestizos; however, provisions that prohibited mestizo priests from saying mass in public or taking confessions considerably reduced the value of the decree.

Despite discrimination, mulattoes, metis, and mestizo contributions to the development of North America have been noteworthy and often quite remarkable. There was, until the late twentieth century, a general failure to recognize the distinctive achievements of the metis, mulattoes, and mestizos. The focus on tolerance of racial diversity has shifted the very important issues of acceptance of people of other races and cooperation between races to the background.

In some cases, this neglect arises from not knowing the facts about race. In addition, much of the writing about race has taken the form of sociopolitical articles directed toward the solution of what some view as a political problem rather than an attempt to understand race and the mixing of races as a culturally enriching situation.

Juana Iris Goergen

José María Morelos y Pavón, a Mexican Roman Catholic priest, was a mestizo who prohibited the use of terms such as Indian, mulatto, and caste to categorize people. He led a revolt against Spanish rule in 1812 and was executed in 1815.

DAILY LIFE

THE METIS IN MANITOBA

The story of the metis, descendants of Indian women and European men involved in the eighteenth- and nineteenth-century fur trade, has been well documented. The metis had adopted a predominantly European material culture by the mid-1800's, and a majority of the anthropologists and historians who have studied metis society characterize it as a hybrid culture, one that integrates European and Indian characteristics. This ethnicity involves a host of intangibles including a sense of common identity founded on and strengthened by historical events of the nineteenth century. Perhaps the most significant of these events, the Red River, or Riel, Rebellions (1869–1870), was caused by the Canadian government's failure to recognize metis land claims.

In negotiations to acquire Hudson's Bay Company holdings, the Canadian government proposed paying compensation to the company and the Native Americans but recognized metis occupation only if the lots were registered with the company. All remaining land was to be surveyed for distribution to immigrants from Ontario. When Canadian land surveyors began taking over metis landholdings, French- and English-speaking metis drew on their experience organizing buffalo hunts to form a provisional government with Louis Riel as their spokesman. Riel was articulate and well educated, and he quickly took charge. First, he took control of the colony by occupying the Hudson's Bay Company stronghold of Fort Gary. Subsequently, on December 8, 1869, he proclaimed the creation of the Red River Republic under a provisional government. Negotiations with the Canadian government focused on issues of land rights and participation in a territorial government.

These issues were resolved in 1870 with the passage of the Manitoba Act. It created the province of Manitoba, a self-governed district with full representation in the federal legislature and senate. It guaranteed separate schools and officially sanctioned the equality of the French and English languages. Most important for the metis, it established a metis land base of 1.4 million acres.

A metis scout pauses while on patrol in 1885 as part of his duties with the North West Mounted Police in Canada.

FURTHER READING

•Burley, David V., Gayel A. Horsfall, and John D. Brandon. *Structural Considerations of Metis Ethnicity.* Vermillion: University of South Dakota Press, 1992.

•MacLachlan, Colin M., and Jaime Rodríguez. *The Forging of the Cosmic Race: A Reinterpretation of Colonial Mexico.* Berkeley: University of California Press, 1980.

•Smith, John David, ed. *Racial Determinism and the Fear of Miscegenation Pre-1900.* Vols. 7-8. New York: Garland Publishing, 1993.

•Williamson, Joel. *New People: Miscegenation and Mulattoes in the United States.* Baton Rouge: Louisiana State University Press, 1995.

TEMPER OF THE TIMES

THE COSMIC RACE

Colonial Mexico was a dynamic society enjoying both a stable government and a prosperous economy. By incorporating Indians, Europeans, Africans, and Asians in a unique cultural mix, colonial Mexico formed a society that differed substantially from its contemporaries. The blending of four ethnic groups in Mexico created a new people, a "cosmic race," as José Vasconcelos, one of Mexico's greatest intellectuals, termed it early in the twentieth century. The cosmic race was the mestizo society and culture that emerged in New Spain. This culture was neither Indian nor European and not entirely homogeneous. A few isolated and somewhat nonintegrated Indian groups remained at one end of the spectrum, and new immigrants from Europe, Africa, and Asia were at the other. Both groups were small and in the process of becoming acculturated to the hybrid mestizo culture that rapidly became dominant. The dominant society was called Mexican, to indicate its mestizo nature.

The creation of a new society in a populated land with an ancient and highly civilized culture required monumental adjustments. The accommodation of race mixtures, historically a very difficult challenge, succeeded in New Spain. The cultural and biological intermingling of Indians, Europeans, Africans, and Asians created a new people and a new society. This success may be attributable in part to the great economic opportunities that emerged in Mexico after the Spanish conquest. Although certain aspects of a racial and caste system appeared initially, New Spain rapidly developed a class structure consonant with an emerging capitalist society. Materialism, competition, and the realization that status and social position rested on economic success engendered great stress as well as opportunity. Governing Mexico's complex society presented a great challenge.

Internal stress and externally imposed reforms in the second half of the eighteenth century upset the relatively autonomous development of New Spain. The resulting social crisis exacerbated race and class conflicts. Changes that were introduced by eighteenth-century Spanish reformers further disrupted the delicate balance of ethnic groups and economic interests that had formed over the years. Only with the violent Revolution of 1910, which resulted in the social and political acceptance of the nation's mestizo culture, was a more positive balance restored.

A family of the so-called cosmic race preparing a meal in Mexico in the eighteenth century. Members of the cosmic race were descended from Indian, European, African, and Asian forebears.

Metacom's War

Beginning on June 20, 1675, settlers in southern New England began to be attacked by local Indians. Initially, these attacks were localized in the Plymouth Colony area and were attributed only to the Wampanoag leader Metacom (King Philip). After delays caused by intercolonial disputes, a militia was formed.

For about the first half of the war, however, colonial records detail only inexperience and loss, ambush after ambush, troop members mistakenly shooting their own men. Ranks of soldiers, ranging from farmers to pirates, were released from jail to learn European battle methodologies, only to be dumbfounded by native strategy.

By July, the war had spread into the Massachusetts Bay Colony as another powerful people, the Nipmucks, joined Metacom. By August, the front had moved into the upper Connecticut Valley. In December, the militia attacked and killed a large number of the then neutral Narragansett to prevent them from joining the war. This campaign boosted morale. The euphoria evaporated, however, as this "great swamp fight" turned into February's "hungry march" and Indian forces, now including the Narragansett, initiated a new offensive.

Although the Indian forces hit their high-water mark in the widely scattered April 1676 attacks, the Pyrrhic victory in mid-May at the Falls of the Connecticut signaled a telling shift. By summer, the colonial militia, having learned to prize the survival, scouting, and ambushing skills of their own Indian advisers, was becoming more and more efficient.

At the same time, small bands of starving, homeless Indians began surrendering, some becoming victims of military (and paramilitary) units bolstered by the weakening of Indian resistance. Metacom was making his way back to his homeland in search of food for his starving people when a force under the direction of Captain Benjamin Church was able to surround and kill him, thus marking the official end of the war.

Anna Dunlap Higgins

A seventeenth-century woodcut of Metacom, the chief of the Wampanoag Indians of New England, who began a war with colonists in 1675.

CAUSES AND EFFECTS

The background of Metacom's War is complex, involving crises within colonies, disputes with England, rivalries between colonies, and worsening settler-Indian relations. One of the causes was the settlers' appropriation of native lands, though problems arose also because settlers insisted that the Indians become Christians and that they adhere to the English judicial and commercial systems, which the Indians viewed as increasingly biased. The war nearly destroyed the colonies physically, economically, and spiritually. In proportion to the population, it was, in fact, one of the deadliest North American wars. The indiscriminate massacres, typical of seventeenth-century European war strategy, and the bounties offered by the militia introduced the concept of extermination to a people previously predisposed to limit war casualties and ended the independent existence and the resistance of Indians in southern New England.

SEE ALSO: BRITISH SETTLEMENT.

Meuse-Argonne Offensive

SEE ALSO:
WILSON'S PRESIDENCY;
WORLD WAR I & THE
U.S.

In September 1918, as part of the general Allied offensive against German forces in France, Marshal Ferdinand Foch assigned the American Expeditionary Force (AEF) to the Meuse-Argonne sector of a line running from Ieper, Belgium, to Verdun, France. The commander of the AEF, General John J. Pershing, commanded two French corps in addition to 600,000 American troops.

Pershing's plan called for an advance of about 6 miles (10 kilometers) by the end of the first day with an advance on the second day to a total of 10 miles (16 kilometers). He believed that he would have the advantage of surprise, which would prevent the Germans from reinforcing before he attacked.

The Americans were superior to the defending Germans in numbers of men and artillery, aircraft, and tanks. Also the troops manning that sector were mainly Saxons and Austro-Hungarians, many of whom had little dedication to the German cause. The German Army did, however, have strong fortifications, and the Argonne Forest acted as a natural defense.

At 5:30 A.M. on September 26, 1918, the American-French forces began their attack. They quickly overran the first German prepared defenses but stalled in the open terrain beyond, the consequence of steady German machine gun fire. By the second day

A commanding officer and men of the 58th U.S. Infantry consult a map as they plan their next move in the Meuse-Argonne Offensive.

the advancing Americans had reached their first goal, but the offensive had run out of steam. Pershing then shifted veteran divisions to the fighting line and rested his troops. When the offensive resumed on October 4, the Germans had reinforced and were more prepared for the attack. Heavy fighting ensued, and the attackers again became bogged down.

On October 14 the tired and ill Americans seized the high ground around Cunel and Romagne-sous-Montfaucon but were too exhausted to continue. The next stage, beginning on November 1, called for Pershing's army to take the heights around Sedan. The advance progressed quickly over the next ten days as the Germans continually retreated. The American pursuit halted only with the November 11 declaration of an armistice ending the war. American casualties totaled 117,000 and the Germans lost more than 100,000.

The Meuse-Argonne Offensive was the largest offensive in which American troops had ever fought and its numbers were not surpassed until 1944.

Michael R. Nichols

Mexican-American War

U.S. troops charge Mexican forces at the Battle of Resaca de Palma on May 9, 1846, during the Mexican-American War.

By 1845, diplomatic relations between Mexico and the United States, which had been deteriorating for years, were broken off completely. Besides the Texas border dispute, the United States had sought reparation for American property lost as a result of Mexico's failure to maintain order in its northern provinces. President James K. Polk, without success, had also been trying to purchase Upper California, but the Mexican government, under President Mariano Paredes y Arrillaga, had indignantly refused to consider any American proposals. Paredes, a centralist, had come to power with the 1845 overthrow and exile of Antonio López de Santa Anna, who was ousted because he had been willing to negotiate with the American government.

AN INEVITABLE WAR

The border dispute was exacerbated by America's expansionist movement, fueled by the concept of manifest destiny, and frustrated by Mexico's diplomatic intransigence (SEE Western Explorations; Westward Expansion). Pressure on Polk to pursue a more aggressive policy mounted, much of it coming from fellow Democrats who, in 1844, when Polk was elected president, had campaigned on the expansionist slogan Fifty-Four Forty or Fight, pressing for annexation of the Northwest Territories. In response to the pressure, Polk sent troops under General Zachary Taylor into the disputed area, deliberately provoking a response.

When Mexican and American patrols skirmished in April 1846, shedding "American blood on American soil," Polk had his excuse to ask Congress to declare war, which it did on May 13. The only real resistance in Senate debates came from Northern abolitionists, who feared an extension of slavery

SUMMARY

➤ Border disputes and expansionist pressures instigated the Mexican-American War in 1846.

➤ Early in the war, General Zachary Taylor achieved victories in northeastern Mexico, and the United States seized control of California and New Mexico.

➤ General Winfield Scott captured Veracruz in March 1847 and took Mexico City in September.

➤ The war, which ended in 1848, gave the United States California, New Mexico, and large parts of present-day Utah, Arizona, Colorado, Nevada, and Wyoming.

CAUSES AND EFFECTS

When Texas became part of the country in 1845, the United States inherited the former republic's border dispute with Mexico. Texas claimed that its southwestern boundary was the Rio Bravo del Norte, and Mexico claimed that it was the Nueces River, much farther to the east. Under pressure from expansionists, who hoped to force Mexico to cede California and New Mexico to the United States, President James Polk declared war when Mexican forces attacked American patrols in the disputed area of Texas. The Treaty of Guadalupe Hidalgo, which ended the war, ceded California and New Mexico to the United States and established the Rio Grande and Gila Rivers as its national boundaries with Mexico. It also left a bitter legacy in Mexican-American relations.

into annexed territory and from constitutional ideologues like Henry Clay and Daniel Webster, who felt Polk had usurped congressional authority by making the war a fait accompli (SEE Missouri Compromise).

EARLY U.S. VICTORIES

The war began in northeastern Mexico even before its formal declaration. Taylor quickly won a series of battles against larger forces, starting with a victory at Palo Alto on May 8. After additional victories at Resaca de la Palma and Matamoros, he laid siege to

General Zachary Taylor sits outside his tent during the Mexican-American War. Taylor was the commander of the U.S. troops for the initial battles of the war.

Monterrey, which fell on September 24. By then, still reeling from internal political turmoil, the Mexican government had ousted President Paredes and given command of the army to Santa Anna, who had just arrived from exile in Cuba, in hopes he could reverse the country's military fortunes. On December 6, the Mexican congress also restored Santa Anna's presidential powers (SEE Santa Anna's Governments).

Santa Anna's return to power failed to achieve its aim. Taylor gained his greatest victory four months after Santa Anna's return, on February 23, 1847, at Buena Vista. Taylor's small force of 4,700 men narrowly defeated Santa Anna's army of 20,000. Similar successes were achieved by forces under the commands of Captain John C. Frémont and Colonel Stephen W. Kearney, who, respectively, seized control of California and New Mexico with almost no casualties (SEE Frémont's Expeditions). Clearly, the United States, guided by its expansionist vision, was interested in the spoils of a war that it believed it would win.

SCOTT TAKES MEXICO CITY

Despite its early defeats, Mexico remained intractable in the face of American demands, and Polk decided to send General Winfield Scott into Mexico to storm the capital, Mexico City, while Taylor was ordered to hold his ground in northeastern Mexico. The move was in part politically motivated by Polk's concern over the increasing popularity of Taylor, who had made no secret of his presidential aspirations.

On March 27, 1847, Scott landed on the Mexican coast. He won an easy victory at Veracruz. This port city was the gateway to the interior and the capital. The capture of

the harbor fortress was important, for it allowed American ships to supply Scott's army on its 250-mile (402 kilometer) trek into the Mexican heartland.

A series of successful battles against larger forces followed. The key battle was fought on April 18, at the pass of Cerro Gordo, where Scott's 8,000-man force routed a 15,000-man Mexican army under Santa Anna. Santa Anna thereafter began secret communications with Scott in an apparent effort to negotiate a separate peace without the knowledge of the Mexican government. He even agreed to an armistice conference with Nicholas Trist, who, at the beginning of Santa Anna's peace overtures, had been sent to Mexico by Secretary of State James Buchanan. The conference, beginning in Tacubaya on August 17, 1847, accomplished nothing except a short truce, and by early September, it had become clear to Scott and Trist that Santa Anna was merely playing for time, hoping disease, declining morale, and supply problems would render Scott's army weak enough to defeat. Scott, meanwhile, continued his triumphant march, winning battles at Jalapa, Perote, Puebla, Contreras, Churubusco, and Molino del Rey. Finally, on

September 13, his troops stormed the fortress at Chapultepec, three miles from the capital. The poorly equipped, disorganized Mexicans were outgunned by the more disciplined, better-led U.S. troops, and they capitulated after a fierce day of fighting. Scott entered Mexico City the following day and began a successful occupation in the face of a brief resistance by the citizenry.

Santa Anna, already facing impeachment for his mismanagement of the war, did not wait for Scott's triumphant entry into the capital. He left the city with a small force of volunteers, planning to engage in guerrilla attacks on Scott's supply lines and lay siege to Puebla, where Scott had set up his headquarters. However, on October 8, near Puebla, Santa Anna was defeated for the last time. Relieved of his command on October 16, he obtained permission from the interim government of Manuel de la Peña y Peña to reenter exile, leaving the command structure of the Mexican army in total collapse and the war at its de facto end.

The formal end, delayed several weeks, came shortly after the treaty negotiations began at Guadalupe Hidalgo on January 2, 1848. The accords fashioned there were

The American naval bombardment of Veracruz in March 1847 weakened the city's defenses. After they had taken a two-day battering from land and from the sea, the Mexican defenders of Veracruz surrendered to General Winfield Scott.

PROFILE

ANTONIO LÓPEZ DE SANTA ANNA (1794–1876)

The Mexican-American War brought the last major downturn in the mercurial career of General Antonio López de Santa Anna, who had been at the center of Mexican military and political affairs for well over two decades. The son of a minor colonial administrator, Santa Anna first served as an officer in the Spanish Army but later fought for Mexican independence against Spain. He quickly proved an ambitious and pragmatic politician, capable of deceit and treachery in both his foreign and domestic policies.

By 1829 he had become very popular, winning great acclaim as the Hero of Tampico in the Mexican struggle against Spanish efforts to reclaim Mexico. His military success led to the presidency in 1833 and his attempts to establish a strong central government. In 1836 he led Mexican forces into Texas in an effort to crush a rebellion of American settlers who had proclaimed their independence from Mexico. Although Santa Anna annihilated the much smaller American force at the Alamo, in the later Battle of San Jacinto (April 21, 1836), against forces led by Sam Houston, he was defeated and captured. After a brief sojourn in Washington, D.C., he was sent back to Mexico by President Andrew Jackson.

He came out of a brief political retirement in 1838, leading an army against French forces that had seized Veracruz in reprisal for alleged injuries done to French nationals in Mexico. The French were withdrawing when Santa Anna's army arrived, so the expedition ended in a very limited engagement, although it cost Santa Anna a leg. For a short time in 1839 he assumed dictatorial powers and two years thereafter led a rebellion and seized the presidency. In 1845, he was again forced into exile.

When war with the United States erupted in 1846, Santa Anna contacted President James Polk, offering to serve as a peace emissary, but upon his return to Mexico took command of the Mexican forces, fighting first against General Zachary Taylor and later against General Winfield Scott. A series of military reversals forced him into exile once more, first to Jamaica and later to New Granada, from where his remaining efforts to broker power in Mexican affairs were largely frustrated. Impoverished and blind, he was allowed to return to his native soil two years before his death in 1876.

General Winfield Scott, whose military victories over Santa Anna's troops forced the Mexican to flee into exile.

ratified by the U.S. Senate on March 10 but were not formally proclaimed until July 4. "Mr. Polk's war," as it came to be known, had cost the United States about 13,000 lives and $100 million in expenses.

TREATY OF GUADALUPE HIDALGO

Mexico had been forced to accept humiliating peace terms (SEE Treaty of Guadalupe Hidalgo). The provisions more fully realized the aims of the American expansionists than those offered by Trist at the earlier, clandestine armistice conference. The area of California ceded to the United States was vast, extending from one nautical league south of San Diego to the Northwest Territories. The Territory of New Mexico, also vast, contained present-day New Mexico and large parts of present-day Utah, Arizona, Colorado, Nevada, and Wyoming. As compensation, the United States agreed to pay Mexico $15 million, to guarantee U.S.

VIEWPOINTS

MANIFEST DESTINY

During the 1840's, manifest destiny became the rallying cry of American expansionists who believed it was the God-given right of the United States to annex all territories between the Atlantic and the Pacific Oceans and to extend the national boundaries farther to the north and south. The term was coined by John L. O'Sullivan, who first used it in his *United States Magazine and Democratic Review* in the summer of 1845. He proclaimed that it was the country's destiny "to over-spread the continent allotted by Providence for the free development of our yearly multiplying millions." The term was quickly picked up and used in congressional deliberations. Although it was a major political credo of the Democrats, some Whigs and Republicans espoused the doctrine as well. The expression was often echoed in debates over the annexation of Texas, the Oregon territorial disputes, and the promotion and prosecution of the war with Mexico. The Republicans also revived the doctrine during the 1890's, when the United States annexed Guam and the Philippines in the negotiated settlement of the Spanish-American War (1898).

citizenship and constitutional rights to Mexican nationals in the ceded territory, and to assume liability for the reparation claims made by American citizens against Mexico. The monetary concessions were a small price to pay for a vast territory that was extremely rich in natural resources, including gold and silver, and a lengthy Pacific coastline that would serve as a gateway to Asia and eventually play a major role in turning the United States into a world power.

John W. Fiero

The Mexican-American War spread from northeastern to southeastern Mexico. The Treaty of Guadalupe Hidalgo, signed at the war's conclusion, saw Mexico cede an enormous swathe of territory in the northwest.

SEE ALSO:
Frémont's Expeditions; Gadsden Purchase; Missouri Compromise; Santa Anna's Governments; Spanish-American War; Treaty of Guadalupe Hidalgo; Western Explorations; Westward Expansion.

FURTHER READING

• Bauer, K. Jack. *The Mexican War, 1846–1848.* New York: Macmillan, 1974.
• Connor, Seymour V., and Odre B. Faulk. *North America Divided: The Mexican War, 1846–1848.* New York: Oxford University Press, 1971.
• Eisenhower, John S. D. *So Far from God: The U.S. War with Mexico, 1846–1848.* New York: Random House, 1989.
• Johannsen, Robert W. *To the Halls of the Montezumas: The Mexican War in the American Imagination.* New York: Oxford University Press, 1985.
• Pletcher, David M. *The Diplomacy of Annexation: Texas, Oregon, and the Mexican War.* Columbia: University of Missouri Press, 1973.
• Schroeder, John H. *Mr. Polk's War.* Madison: University of Wisconsin Press, 1973.
• Weems, John E. *To Conquer a Peace: The War Between the United States and Mexico.* Garden City, N.Y.: Doubleday, 1974.

Legend:
- US-Mexico border 1846
- US-Mexico border 1848
- Land ceded to US by the Treaty of Guadalupe Hidalgo

Mexican Constitution of 1857

Benito Juárez, as president of Mexico, developed and added to the liberties afforded by the Mexican Constitution of 1857.

The Mexican liberal constitution was set up by a constituent congress in February 1857. It was designed to introduce Mexico to liberal democracy. Throughout the 1850's, tension had been brewing between the liberals and conservatives and, consequently, between the church and state. The Catholic Church was conservative, and the liberals were associated with the rising interests of the state. All Mexican public officials were required to swear allegiance to the constitution of 1857. The Church, which was against the document, excommunicated individuals who took the oath. The constitution guaranteed many civil liberties and restricted the power of the president, an office that had often been abused.

The liberals wanted to destroy the religious foundation of Mexico by promoting secular education and economic liberalism. The constitution was a thorn in the side of the president, Ignacio Comonfort. The president was caught in the middle of the liberal-conservative struggle, and his indecision led to his leaving the Mexican government in early 1858. After Comonfort, Benito Juárez, an Indian lawyer, became constitutional president (SEE Juárez Government).

During his presidency, the government issued laws that furthered the liberal motives of the constitution. These laws brought about the separation of church and state, the seizure and nationalization of the church's property, the abolition of tithes (an instrumental source of income for the Catholic Church), and the suppression of religious corporations. The period known as La Reforma began with the 1857 constitution and continued through the subsequent three-year War of the Reform that ended in a liberal victory. After the victory, however, the liberals still faced many obstacles in attempting to advance the socioeconomic and political well-being of Mexico.

David Trevino

CAUSES AND EFFECTS

After the rule of Antonio López de Santa Anna ended in the mid-1850's, the liberals became more prominent in Mexico. They began to enact laws that reflected their political philosophy, such as the Ley Juárez and the Ley Lerdo, which reduced the social, economic, and political power of the Catholic Church in Mexico. The constitution of 1857 embodied many of the liberals' ideas. It strengthened the congress to prevent the president from abusing his power, and it contained measures intended to weaken the Church, thereby intensifying the conflict between church and state.

The period known as La Reforma, which began with the 1857 constitution and continued after Benito Juárez became president in 1858, highlighted the political and economic troubles plaguing Mexico. The reforms created instability and economic problems and paved the way for foreign intervention on the part of France, Britain, and Spain, which culminated in the rule of Maximilian I of Mexico.

SEE ALSO: JUÁREZ GOVERNMENT; MEXICAN REPUBLIC; SANTA ANNA'S GOVERNMENTS.

Mexican Constitution of 1917

Early in the twentieth century, a variety of groups united to remove President Porfirio Díaz from power (SEE Díaz Regime), then splintered, and Mexico lapsed into the chaotic Mexican Revolution (1910–1920; SEE Mexican Revolution). By late 1916, Venustiano Carranza's faction seemed the strongest, and to solidify his legitimacy as rightful ruler, Carranza ordered that a convention meet in November 1916 to draft a new constitution.

Although Carranza invited more conservative than liberal delegates, the constitution created was far more liberal than he intended. The 1917 constitution sharply increased the government's role in society and limited the Catholic Church's power. The constitution went into effect on February 5, 1917.

The 1917 constitution attempted to improve the living conditions of specific groups in Mexican society, especially the poor. Article 123 provided amazingly liberal reforms for urban laborers, such as an eight-hour workday, workers' compensation, and the right to organize and strike. The land reform program in Article 27 tried to help peasant farmers by promising to return lands to peasant villages that had been taken by large ranches, limiting the amount of land that foreign companies could own, and decreasing the size of ranches owned by the wealthy. Article 27 also established subsoil rights for Mexico, meaning that anything below Mexican soil, such as oil and minerals, was the property of the nation and could not be taken from the country without the government's permission.

The constitution also sought to limit the power and influence of the Catholic Church by ending its control over education. Instead of church schools, the government promised free, secular, and universal education, meaning that all children, not just those of the rich, could attend. The constitution also limited the Church's power by forbidding the Church from owning land, and in order to separate church and state, public officials could no longer openly declare their religion.

William Bridges

General Venustiano Carranza was elected president of Mexico in May 1917. He failed to implement the radical Constitution created earlier that year.

CAUSES AND EFFECTS

The Mexican constitution of 1857 had not addressed many basic issues in Mexican society, and the constitutional assembly in 1916 tried to solve those issues by making the government more responsive to the needs of the lower classes. The constitution of 1917 was the result. Unlike most Latin American countries, Mexico has not experienced a revolution or military takeover since the constitution's creation, in part because of the constitution's promises for all Mexicans.

These social commitments included labor and land reforms designed to improve the living conditions of the lower class and place limits on the power of the Catholic Church. Many presidents did not implement the reforms but were careful not to create the impression that they were defying the constitution. President Lázaro Cárdenas (1934–1940) was the first to implement many of the reforms.

SEE ALSO: CÁRDENAS GOVERNMENT; DÍAZ REGIME; MEXICAN CONSTITUTION OF 1857; MEXICAN REVOLUTION.

Mexican Immigration to the North

A Mexican immigrant at work picking cotton in Arizona in 1943. Throughout the twentieth century, Mexico has been a constant source of cheap, hardworking labor for employers in the United States.

SUMMARY

➤ Mexican immigrants initially settled in California, Arizona, New Mexico, Texas, and Nevada, regions originally part of Mexico.
➤ The first wave of immigrants, about 219,000 people, came during the Mexican Revolution, between 1911 and 1920.
➤ The 1920's brought 480,576 more immigrants, seeking improved economic opportunities.
➤ More than seven million Mexicans immigrated to the United States between 1940 and 1960, many participating in the bracero program.
➤ Many Mexicans, drawn by economic opportunities, have illegally immigrated to the United States.

The number of Mexican immigrants to the United States has remained a matter of sophisticated guesswork because of a lack of precise data from the nineteenth century and the confusion of census takers in the twentieth century. What is certain is that Mexican immigrants initially settled in the five southwestern states of California, Arizona, New Mexico, Texas, and Nevada. The Southwest was hospitable to Mexican immigrants because it was a region where Spanish was commonly spoken, Mexican communities had long existed, and their labor was needed.

Mexican immigration to the United States is a complicated issue because the region with the heaviest Mexican population was originally part of Mexico. Before the Texas Revolution and the Mexican-American War, Mexico had held the Southwest since Francisco Vásquez de Coronado claimed the lands for Spain in 1540. Many Mexican settlements existed in the Southwest, mainly in Texas and California.

In Mexico, the hacienda, or privately owned estate, became the basis for social organization. To function, the hacienda needed labor. *Hacendados*, or the owners of haciendas, invited workers to settle on or near the estates. Indians and poor Spaniards accepted, becoming virtual slaves. This feudal system would eventually provide the reason for civil war in Mexico and mass migration northward to the United States (SEE Hacienda Plantation System). Emigrants headed for lands that had recently belonged to Mexico.

Early Mexican pueblos such as San Antonio (1718), San Jose (1777), and Los Angeles (1781) had by 1820 become bustling agricultural and trading centers. The immense flow of immigrants from the United States and Europe, who were attracted by the lucrative trade between these communities and the Ohio Valley, worried the Mexican government, but it was too late to staunch the tide of settlers.

Initially, the immigrants to what is now the Southwest were American settlers who came at the invitation of Mexico. People such as Moses Austin and his son Stephen F. Austin answered the call for the settlement of Texas. By 1835, between 25,000 and 35,000 American, but only 5,000 Mexican, settlers lived throughout Texas. Likewise, California had become the ultimate goal for American expansionists, who desired its seaports and were attracted to real and imagined opportunities.

The Texas Revolution in 1835, although initially a joint enterprise between Americans and Mexicans living in Texas, ultimately led to the formation of the border and the closing off of the Southwest to Mexican citizens (SEE Texas Revolution). The creation of the border did not, however, end the familial and regional ties that Mexicans had with the Southwest, and border crossing became widely practiced. Despite the guarantees of the Treaty of Guadalupe Hidalgo, which ended the

A food vendor at the Fiesta Tejano in San Antonio, Texas. Tacos, tortillas, and other foods introduced by Mexican immigrants are now familiar to all Americans.

DAILY LIFE

FAMILY LIFE IN SAN ANTONIO

San Antonio is one of the oldest cities in the United States, and its character has been influenced heavily by its residents of Mexican ancestry. The city's five missions stand witness to early Mexican settlements. The most famous mission, the Alamo, is the most visited historical site in Texas. San Antonio's downtown is crisscrossed by the San Antonio River with its historical Riverwalk, where many fine Mexican restaurants are located. El Mercado provides a quadrangle in which numerous fiestas are held and where mariachi and tejano music can be heard every weekend. The most anticipated event in San Antonio is Fiesta Week in March, which celebrates the city's history and diversity and pays homage to its Mexican roots. During Fiesta Week, the River and Battle of Flowers Parades are held, and downtown San Antonio is the site for three celebrations: Semana Allegre, Night in Old San Antonio, and the carnival. More than 100,000 people crowd the city streets, and hundreds of food booths sell a wide variety of ethnic foods.

Mexicans who had waded across the Rio Grande to enter the United States illegally are taken off a freight train in Los Angeles in 1953. These men had hidden under a shipment of pipes inside one of the compartments.

formed previously useless land into highly profitable agricultural regions.

The building of the railroad during the post-Civil War era (SEE Transcontinental Railroad) provided access to eastern markets. This created, by the end of the century, an economic system that was based on farms owned by Euroamericans and worked by Mexican Americans. Southwest farms needed workers. The Mexican Revolution provided the labor force.

The opposition to Porfirio Díaz' rule led by Emiliano Zapata and Francisco Madero came to a head on May 24, 1911, when Díaz was forced to resign (SEE Díaz Regime; Mexican Revolution). The turmoil continued, however, and hundreds of thousands of Mexican citizens were displaced.

The majority of the immigrants were peasants who had been bound to the lands controlled by the *hacendados*. Nearly 10 percent of Mexico's population emigrated during the Mexican Revolution. By 1925, Los Angeles was home to the largest community of Mexicans outside of Mexico City.

Until the mid-1920's, the border was not controlled (SEE Border Life). The Border Patrol was not formed until 1924, and, therefore, the exact number of Mexican immigrants is unknown. Some estimates suggest that approximately 77,000 Mexicans emigrated between 1820 and 1910.

The influx of immigrants between 1911 and 1920 is estimated at 219,000. The number of immigrants from Mexico during the revolutionary period was three times what it had been in the ninety years before that chaotic decade.

The next decade saw the number of immigrants more than double, growing to 480,576. As immigrants entered the agricultural workforce and began to enjoy an

Mexican-American War and ceded much of the Southwest to the United States (SEE Treaty of Guadalupe Hidalgo), Mexican-American citizens were largely denied their land claims. Euro-American immigrants and settlers tried to reduce the population of Mexican Americans and native Indians to cheap laborers. Irrigation projects in east Texas and California's Central Valley trans-

CAUSES AND EFFECTS

Most of the Mexican immigration to the United States can be attributed to either displacement due to domestic unrest or adverse economic conditions. For example, the Mexican recession in 1981 led to an increased level of illegal immigration. As long as the disparity between the Mexican and U.S. economies exists, immigration will continue.

As the American economy evolves, controversy probably will continue to surround the effects of immigration on the U.S. economy. The 1990's have given rise to several anti-immigration bills and laws that have attempted to strip both legal and illegal immigrants of medical, educational, and social benefits and civil protection.

VIEWPOINTS

ECONOMIC IMPACT OF ILLEGAL IMMIGRANTS

The issue of what illegal immigration costs taxpayers has been hotly debated. Some claim that illegal immigrants are taxing the overburdened social safety net. Others assert that although many children of undocumented workers use the public education system, that cost is offset by the taxes that are collected up front from undocumented workers' paychecks; although those workers have a legal right to a tax refund, their fear of being deported dissuades them from filing tax returns. Mexican and other undocumented workers also pay a great deal of money into the social security fund, yet they can never collect from it; they use few, if any, public services and, as a group, more than pay their way.

On the other side of the argument, George Borjas, an economics professor at the University of California at San Diego, claims that the twenty million immigrants in the United States receive $1.1 billion more in welfare payments than they pay into the welfare system through taxes. In rebuttal, others argue that immigrants, both legal and illegal, are inclined to use their wages on goods and services in the United States and actually contribute $5 billion annually to the economy through local and state sales taxes. This translates to a net gain of $4 billion.

Cornell University labor economist Vernon Briggs, however, argues that the influx of unskilled workers from Mexico and other nations is displacing American workers from an already shrinking unskilled labor market. The counterargument, offered by scholar James Cockcroft and others, is that Briggs' theory mistakenly assumes that there are unskilled workers in the United States willing to work in menial jobs. The argument has also been made that problems in the American economy cannot be blamed on illegal immigration. Wade Henderson of the National Association for the Advancement of Colored People suggests that the change from an industrial economy to a high-technology and service-oriented economy is to blame for displacing American workers.

Studies conducted by the Urban Institute have found that immigrants boost overall employment. The institute found that for every hundred-person increase in the adult immigrant population, forty-six new jobs are created, almost double the number of jobs per hundred-person increase in the adult population of native-born Americans. The debate will persist as new legislation is enacted and as the influx of both documented and undocumented immigrants continues.

A U.S. Border Patrol agent looks through a pair of binoculars to scan the border between the United States and Mexico.

FURTHER READING

•Cockcroft, James D. *Outlaws in the Promised Land: Mexican Immigrant Workers and America's Future*. New York: Grove Press, 1986.

•Gamio, Manuel. *Mexican Immigration to the United States*. New York: Dover, 1971.

•Hondagneu-Sotelo, Pierrette. *Gendered Transitions: Mexican Experiences of Immigration*. Berkeley: University of California Press, 1994.

improved standard of living, their fellow nationals decided to move north to escape poverty and Mexico's stagnant economy. As the labor market in the Southwest became glutted, many workers continued northward into the Midwest and Pacific Northwest.

During the Great Depression, there was a period of "repatriation" during which Mexican workers, many of whom had become citizens, were deported and the level of legal immigration fell to fewer than 23,000 entries during the 1930's. Anti-Mexican

(Continued on page 778)

FURTHER READING

•Mills, Nicolaus, ed. *Arguing Immigration: The Debate over the Changing Face of America.* New York: Touchstone, 1994.

•Mouquin, Wayne. *A Documentary History of the Mexican Americans.* New York: Praeger, 1971.

•Perez, Ramon T. *Diary of an Undocumented Immigrant.* Houston: Arte Público Press, 1991.

•Ramsdell, Charles. *San Antonio: A Historical and Pictorial Guide.* Austin: University of Texas Press, 1959.

•Samora, Julian, and Patricia V. Simon. *A History of the Mexican American People.* Notre Dame, Ind.: University of Notre Dame Press, 1977.

hysteria erupted in the country as American workers displaced by the Depression and the Dust Bowl in the southern plains blamed immigrant workers for their misfortune (SEE Dust Bowl, Great Depression).

After the United States entered World War II, the economy recovered, and the labor shortage required that American growers and industry find a cheap, temporary workforce. This gave birth to the bracero program (1942–1964), through which more than five million workers would be brought to the United States over the next twenty years (SEE Bracero Program). The number of illegal immigrants also continued to grow as agribusiness sought to keep wages low by employing undocumented workers. The total number of immigrants from Mexico to the United States between 1940 and 1960 has been estimated at more than seven million.

The number of Mexican immigrants who have entered the United States illegally is a subject of debate. Nearly nine million illegal immigrants were apprehended between 1924 and 1975, but this number reflects only those who were caught. It is clear that the number of illegal immigrants continues to be high, as the population grows and as the Mexican economy fails to provide enough employment for its workers.

Mexico suffered a series of recessions and only partial recoveries in the 1980's and 1990's. Despite anti-immigration initiatives and laws, illegal immigration has continued because undocumented workers readily find work in service and agricultural industries. Immigration has shifted toward urban centers such as Los Angeles and Houston, where work is found in the service industry and in semiskilled jobs in urban industries.

The Hispanic population in the United States rose to more than fourteen million in 1980 and almost doubled by 1994, growing to just over twenty-six million. Census projections predict that the Hispanic population will grow to eighty-one million by the middle of the twenty-first century, representing 21 percent of the U.S. population. Such explosive growth is in large part due to the immigration of Mexicans searching for a better life in the United States. It is an exchange that has added much to the national culture while historically benefiting the U.S. economy.

Manuel Luis Martinez

A tilework mural covers a wall in the El Mercado Market Place in San Antonio, Texas. The mural depicts Mexican musicians and street vendors at market.

Mexican Muralists

The Mexican muralists of the 1920's were both products of the 1910 Revolution and contributors to the proliferation of the revolutionary spirit (SEE Mexican Revolution). Murals appeared on schools, churches, museums, government buildings, and palaces. They brought a new vision to the people of Mexico, portraying their contemporary plight as well as their tumultuous past.

The rebellion against the regime of Porfirio Díaz in 1910 initiated a resurgence of murals in Mexico throughout the turbulent decade (SEE Díaz Regime). In 1920, after the success of the revolution and the beginning of the presidency of revolutionary leader lvaro Obregón, the government officially sanctioned murals and even subsidized their production (SEE Sonora Dynasty).

The tradition of mural painting existed in Mexico long before the advent of the Spanish conquistadors. Vivid murals adorned the buildings of the abandoned Mayan city of

A detail from José Clemente Orozco's mural Miguel Hidalgo, *which is displayed at the Government Palace, Guadalajara.*

Chichén Itzá when it was discovered by Europeans in the late nineteenth century (SEE Mayan Civilization; Spanish Conquest). The methods used to create these artworks were lost or destroyed over the centuries, so the modern murals of revolutionary Mexico were created using European artistic concepts and modern techniques. The new muralists did attempt to capture a sense of Mexico's history, however, by depicting its preconquest past and its indigenous civilizations.

THE MODERN MURALIST

The muralists also used their art to express the Marxist influences and proletarian values popular among many in the intelligentsia at this time, when the young Soviet Union was idealized. The images rejected what the

SUMMARY

➤ The Mexican muralists of the 1910's and 1920's used the mural to portray their political beliefs.
➤ The three most famous muralists, known as the Big Three, are Diego Rivera, José Clemente Orozco, and David Alfaro Siqueiros.
➤ The work of these muralists incorporated European influences and Mexican themes, resulting in a unique art form.
➤ The muralists' influence can be seen today in a resurgence of public art along freeways, on walls, and on skyscrapers.

Peasant followers of Emiliano Zapata and Pancho Villa during the Mexican Revolution are portrayed vividly in this mural by David Alfaro Siqueiros.

CAUSES AND EFFECTS

The Revolution of 1910 ignited the spark of political activism that is so apparent in the work of the Mexican muralists of the 1920's. These murals express the plight of Mexican peasants and of industrial laborers worldwide and depict the world being carried into the twentieth century by the labor of the disenfranchised classes. In depicting the revolutionary spirit of the era, the muralists of Mexico actually contributed to the strength of that spirit by providing a medium for its expression. By popularizing the art form that carried this message, the muralists spread the message as well.

artists perceived as a corrupt and unjust capitalist system, emphasizing instead the importance of united effort, community organization, and common goals.

The mural movement was dominated by three artists: Diego Rivera, José Clemente Orozco, and David Alfaro Siqueiros. The Big Three were highly sophisticated artists who applied their formal training in traditional and contemporary European art to the sociopolitical content of Mexican murals.

The Mexican muralists embraced the positivist method in their work. Rivera, Orozco, Siqueiros, and other artists adhered to the positivist technique of scientific investigation, which emphasized organic and mechanistic functions. The murals demonstrate a fascination with gears, cogs, tubes, and the compartmentalization of industrial life. The muralists portrayed the modern laborer as the embodiment of the human machine. Furthermore, these artists believed that in going through the process of artistic creation, they became components of the greater organism of society. Despite their adherence to positivism, most artists rejected the conservative political message of its credo, Liberty, Order, and Progress, opting instead for what the artists considered to be a more progressive Marxist ideology.

CUBISM AND DUALITY

Many muralists incorporated certain elements of the new Parisian cubist style into their work. They designed their works to accommodate the structural context of public spaces and buildings. Also, the recurrent use of panels, compartments, and other geometric forms demonstrates a fundamental reliance on the cubist style despite the realistic portrayal of figures.

The ancient Mexican belief in a system of duality can be seen in many murals of this era. The indigenous people believed in a system of opposing forces that maintained balance on the earth and within the universe. Dualities such as good and evil, life and death, and heaven and earth prevail in the traditional indigenous religious beliefs. Quetzalcoatl, the divine feathered serpent, represented the antagonistic forces of matter and spirit. Artists such as Rivera extended this concept into the modern era by depicting the opposing forces of the economically disparate Northern and Southern Hemispheres, the politically divided East and

West, developed industry and primitive agriculture, and good and bad government.

THE BIG THREE

Diego Rivera (1886–1957) is the best known Mexican muralist. His frescoes and murals grace the walls of innumerable public buildings throughout the world. Perhaps the most controversial of Rivera's murals was one commissioned by John D. Rockefeller for the Rockefeller Center in New York City in 1933. An ardent fan of Rivera's work, Rockefeller followed the development of the mural enthusiastically until it was brought to his attention that Lenin was depicted in one panel. Rockefeller contended that this image would be too controversial for a public mural, particularly one in this location. The debate over the inclusion of Lenin developed into a power struggle between Rivera and his patron. Ultimately, Rockefeller refused to accept Lenin, and the mural was painted over. Rivera returned to Mexico City, where he re-created the mural at the National Palace, complete with Lenin's face.

Like Rivera, José Clemente Orozco (1883–1949) used his talent to express his Marxist political views. He depicted the plight of the proletariat and the unification and cooperation of people across ethnic and national boundaries. In the positivist style, Orozco portrayed Mexican society as a living entity composed of different segments of society. In an effort not to focus only on what he perceived to be the negative aspects of modern industrial society, Orozco created images of alternative societies. He painted the indigenous people of Mexico and their history, incorporating geometric Christ figures and creation scenes inspired by the great murals and frescoes of the Renaissance, always implying hope for a brighter future.

David Alfaro Siqueiros (1896–1974) began his artistic career with a political objective. At the age of fifteen, he participated in protests, student strikes, and political conspiracies. While studying in Europe, he met Rivera, who, along with several European artists, significantly influenced the development of his style. Although Siqueiros and Rivera disagreed politically, both chose to return to Mexico to re-create Mexico's

past and present in their murals. Though Siqueiros adopted much Aztec and Olmec imagery in his work, he warned artists not to simply reconstruct traditional art but instead to draw upon its energy and style to generate a new indigenous art form.

The Mexican muralists were a group of artists striving to express their political beliefs in an era of turmoil. These muralists contributed not only to an art form and their homeland but also to the worldwide expression of political thought through public art.

Margaret C. Gonzalez

TEMPER OF THE TIMES

THE BILLIONAIRES

In the mural *Modern Industry*, Diego Rivera depicts the modern industrial environment as a labyrinthine factory, honeycombed by compartments. In one compartment, executives conduct a board meeting, while depersonalized laborers toil in the others.

The various compartments are connected by tubes, which extract gold coins from the workers' sections and deposit them in the cubicle of *The Billionaires*, a panel portraying industrial giants J. D. Rockefeller and J. P. Morgan. Rivera clearly used this mural to make a political statement about the negative effects of capitalism, which he saw as exploiting the masses in order to make a few wealthy men even richer.

SEE ALSO:
Aztec Empire; Díaz Regime; Industrial Revolution; Mayan Civilization; Mesoamerican Civilizations; Mexican Revolution; Sonora Dynasty; Spanish Conquest.

FURTHER READING

•Ades, Dawn. *Art in Latin America*. New Haven, Conn.: Yale University Press, 1989.
•Hurlburt, Laurance P. *The Mexican Muralists in the United States*. Albuquerque: University of New Mexico Press, 1989.
•Rivera, Diego, and Bertram D. Wolfe. *Portrait of Mexico*. New York: Covici-Friede, 1937.

J. P. Morgan, John D. Rockefeller, and Henry Ford are among the American industrialists who are shown in Night of the Rich, *a mural by Diego Rivera.*

Mexican Republic

Antonio López de Santa Anna (pointing) led Mexican forces in resisting a Spanish invasion in 1829. The general subseqently came to dominate Mexican politics for three decades.

SUMMARY

➤ Mexico's 1824 constitution reflected the views of liberals and federalists.
➤ Antonio López de Santa Anna took control in 1832 and dominated the political scene for three decades.
➤ The 1857 constitution strengthened the role of the presidency and lessened those of the clergy and military.
➤ Mexico's inability to pay its foreign debt led to a French invasion from 1862 to 1867.
➤ Porfirio Díaz, president from 1878 to 1911, tamed the military, compromised with church officials, and created economic growth.
➤ The Mexican Revolution (1910–1920) changed attitudes, and the 1917 constitution promised social reforms.
➤ Lázaro Cárdenas, president from 1934 to 1940, implemented some social reforms but then focused on creating capital.

After the collapse of Augustín de Iturbide's empire in 1823, a three-member junta governed Mexico on a provisional basis. The first task of the junta was to call elections for a new congress. Regional leaders favored a new congress because the deputies from each state would have administrative control over their domains. This would enable local landowners to control state legislatures. The desire for regional control was national in sentiment, and therefore it did not take long for congress to proclaim a federalist republic after elections took place. The problem of attempting to create an independent republic from colonial and monarchical traditions, however, would be difficult to surmount. Conservatives would continue to argue for a strong central state, and moderates feared the rise of mass politics. Liberals and federalists prevailed, however, and the new constitution reflected their views.

The political system outlined by the 1824 constitution did not always reflect Mexican realities. The struggle between the elites and the masses to control the affairs of government would manifest itself in several decades of uprisings led by generals and deputies. The founding fathers of the Mexican republic were brilliant leaders except for their inability to compromise. The 1828 election signaled the beginning of a seven-year struggle for stability. Manuel Gómez Pedraza won the election, but his defeated rival, Vicente Guerrero, revolted and ousted him before the year ended. Gómez Pedraza then became the head of the moderate faction of the liberals, who opposed the federalists. The populist Guerrero fell in 1829 to centralist leader Anastasio Bustamante, whom the opportunistic Antonio López de Santa Anna overthrew in 1832.

Political disorder arose partially from the inability of the conservative, moderate, and federalist factions to create agreement on economic policy. The issue of free trade split all three factions. Conservatives wanted to construct a domestic, self-sufficient economy, and the moderates and federalists sought European and U.S. products. Provincial economic patterns played an important role as a motivating factor for federalism.

The Mexican War of Independence (1821) had left much of Mexico in economic ruin (SEE Mexican War of Independence). By 1830, economies in several regions had recovered, but the national government still struggled to obtain revenue, and efforts to tax provincial wealth only generated suspicion in northern and southern states. Not surprisingly, those states that prospered became the most ardent federalists.

SANTA ANNA'S FALL

Santa Anna's decision to establish a centralized dictatorship in late 1835 provoked revolts throughout the country. Texas and Yucatán declared their independence, and the inability of Santa Anna to defeat the Texans led to his exile. With the centralists discredited, moderates and federalists controlled Mexico as war with the United States approached in 1845. The stunning defeat of Mexico by the United States resulted in Santa Anna's returning to power shortly after the treaty handed over half the country's territory to the United States. Santa Anna failed miserably, however, and finally was thrown out in 1855 (SEE Santa Anna's Governments).

The liberals decided to reinterpret the realities of Mexican political life. By means of the 1857 constitution (SEE Mexican Constitution of 1857), they abolished the post of vice president and strengthened the presidency. They also ended the privileges of the military and clergy. Federalists, and to a lesser degree moderates, believed that a militia system under local control should exist. The national army, however, distrusted the militia. The army began to pay more attention to regional autonomy than national unity, and partisan rancor polarized the officer corps, promoting dissension and retarding military professionalization. Army cohesion and civilian political ascendancy suffered further when territorial authority was vested in commandants general, whose decentralized commands became largely autonomous fiefdoms. The liberals believed

that free-trade policies would stimulate the economy, which had not performed well except for a brief period in the early 1840's. The liberals also advocated an intense anticlericalism that eventually resulted in the sale of church land as well as indigenous communal holdings.

Domestic strife and internal warfare weakened the economy, and this, in turn, denied the national government sufficient revenues to pay its foreign debt. Because of the government's failure to pay its debt, French emperor Napoleon III attempted to take over Mexico. Although Benito Pablo Juárez fought off French intervention from 1862 to 1867, U.S. support was the key to his success (SEE Juárez Government). The liberals had succeeded in reducing privileges, but religious turmoil, poor economic performance, and political unrest resulted in demands for a new political formula.

Emperor Napoleon III of France attempted to seize control of Mexico from 1862 to 1867.

LAWS AND CASES

THE CONSTITUTION OF 1824

Mexico's Constitution of 1824 was basically a reflection of liberal and federalist thinking, although it conceded several areas to the centralists. The chief liberal, Miguel Ramos Arizpe, presented the congress with a working document modeled upon the Constitution of the United States.

The constitution that eventually emerged, however, followed closely the 1812 constitution, which had been proclaimed during the struggle for independence. The 1812 constitution enjoyed great popularity because of its extreme federalism in terms of allowing local regions to control areas away from the national capital.

The 1824 constitution established the Estados Unidos Mexicanos (united states of Mexico) as a federalist entity made up of nineteen states and four territories. The separation-of-powers clause defining the authority of executive, legislative, and judicial branches reflects the influence of the United States. The legislature also became bicameral, with the senate as the upper house and the chamber of deputies as the lower house. Two senators represented each state, and one deputy spoke for every eighty thousand inhabitants.

What made the document popular in the early republic was its federalist emphasis. The president was to be elected by the state legislatures, as were the senators and the vice president. Primary power was given to the national legislature; the president had little actual power. The landed elites exercised real power, and they received authority to seize communal and public lands.

The centralists persuaded congress to have Catholicism mandated as the only religion. The 1824 constitution, which reflected elite desires to control the masses, said nothing about equality before the law. It also allowed the president to assume extraordinary powers during national emergencies and made the clergy and military exempt from civil courts.

Under Porfirio Díaz (SEE Díaz Regime), Mexico enjoyed great stability from 1876 to 1911. As the country's most outstanding army leader, Díaz tamed the military. This period, known as Porfiriato, was one of tremendous economic growth. Unlike the liberals, Díaz offered tariff protection to industrialists while at the same time encouraging large-scale foreign investment. Regional leaders continued to seize indigenous landholdings as well as large tracts of undeveloped public lands. Perhaps the wisest decision of Díaz was his much-needed compromise with church officials.

Despite these problems, the Church still enjoyed tremendous mass support. Mexican *retablo* (altar-piece) paintings became very popular in the early nineteenth century. These paintings were an integral part of Mexican Catholicism and displayed a distinct synthesis of Christianity and pre-Columbian indigenous beliefs. Because of the popularity of the Church, Díaz worked out a secret agreement with church officials. Anticlerical legislation would remain but not be enforced. Clerical appointments had to meet with Díaz' approval. Díaz kept clerical influence out of the state schools but allowed the Church to maintain its own classrooms. In addition, Díaz quieted those who wanted to reform the Church and permitted religious institutions to accumulate property. With its wealth growing, the Church preached obedience to Díaz and his regime.

The Mexican Revolution (1910–1920) changed the outlook of the republic consid-

Plutarco Elías Calles became president of Mexico in 1924. He instituted widespread public works schemes and led a campaign to undermine the position of the Roman Catholic church in the country.

erably (SEE Mexican Revolution). With the end of the Porfirian order, efforts to improve the lot of the indigenous population grew. Nationalistic attempts to limit foreign investment also had wide popular support. Although the government remained authoritarian, the 1917 constitution (SEE Mexican Constitution of 1917) promised a panacea of social reforms while retaining the anticlericalism of the 1857 constitution.

The decisive turning point of twentieth-century Mexico came during the presidency of Lázaro Cárdenas, 1934–1940 (SEE Cárdenas Government). Designated to become president by the strong-willed Plutarco Elías Calles, the powerful leader of Mexico during the 1920's, Lázaro Cárdenas seemed to be intent upon promoting the ideals of the 1917 constitution by encouraging government-backed strikes and giving large quantities of land to peasants. His educational policies even promoted socialism. The Cárdenas regime also attempted to limit or outlaw gambling, the consumption and manufacture of alcoholic beverages, and prostitution. In 1937, however, the effects of the Great Depression began to be felt in Mexico. Cárdenas began to back off from land and labor reforms, and instead of emphasizing the redistribution of wealth, he began to encourage the creation of capital. New industries appeared, which benefited from Cárdenas' expropriation of oil operations in the country in 1938.

Since 1940, Mexico has attempted to forge a new interpretation of the original republican outlook. Elections have increasingly allowed the appearance of opposition

Tourists climbing a Mayan pyramid at Chichén Itzá. The tourist industry is an important source of revenue for Mexico.

CAUSES AND EFFECTS

After three centuries of increasingly authoritarian colonial rule by Spain, Mexicans rose up in opposition to Madrid from 1810 to 1821 and succeeded in establishing an independent empire under Agustín de Iturbide. Iturbide, however, became increasingly despotic, and regional leaders forced his resignation. During the nineteenth century, the Mexican republic passed through a series of phases, each one providing more power to a national state. During the twentieth century, authoritarianism remained a political reality, but a nationalistic populism provided stability. The desire of regions to exercise more self-rule would never fade away.

SEE ALSO:
CÁRDENAS
GOVERNMENT; DÍAZ
REGIME; THE FRENCH
IN MEXICO; JUÁREZ
GOVERNMENT;
MEXICAN-AMERICAN
WAR; MEXICAN
CONSTITUTION OF
1857; MEXICAN
CONSTITUTION OF
1917; MEXICAN
REVOLUTION; MEXICAN
WAR OF INDEPENDENCE;
SANTA ANNA'S
GOVERNMENTS.

FURTHER READING

•Costeloe, Michael P. *The Central Republic in Mexico, 1835–1846: Hombres de Bien in the Age of Santa Anna.* Cambridge, England: Cambridge University Press, 1993.
•Green, Stanley C. *The Mexican Republic: The First Decade, 1823–1832.* Pittsburgh: University of Pittsburgh Press, 1987.
•Hale, Charles A. *The Transformation of Liberalism in Late Nineteenth Century Mexico.* Princeton, N.J.: Princeton University Press, 1990.
•Rodriguez, Jaime E., ed. *Mexico in the Age of Democratic Revolution, 1750–1850.* Boulder, Colo.: Lynne Reinner, 1994.
•Sinkin, Richard N. *The Mexican Reforma, 1855–1876.* Austin: University of Texas Press, 1979.
•Smith, Robert F. *The United States and Revolutionary Nationalism in Mexico, 1916–1932.* Chicago: University of Chicago Press, 1972.

TEMPER OF THE TIMES

THE CATHOLIC CHURCH

The Catholic Church enjoyed tremendous power during the colonial period. Priests and monks baptized millions of indigenous Mexicans in a successful conversion campaign. The Church effectively amalgamated indigenous beliefs into traditional Catholicism. The prospect of salvation attracted many indigenous peoples, who endured hard earthly lives.

The Catholic Church also provided education, recreation, artistic opportunities, and protection from landowners and plantation owners. The missionaries were led by exceptional friars in the north and south; and two priests led the early phase of the Mexican independence movement.

After independence, the anticlerical liberals began to gain power. Many of the middle class now considered the Church greedy and oppressive. By 1850, church capital amounted to 100 million pesos with another 50 million in income-earning investments. This capital represented a quarter of Mexico's total wealth. The Church also owned considerable real estate, including half the property in Mexico City. Moreover, the Church opposed secular education but did not provide adequate educational facilities. Services remained expensive. For commoners, the cost of a baptism often represented five months of labor; marriage and burial expenses were equally high.

The imposing church of Santa Prisca, Taxco, was completed in 1758. Such buildings reflect the wealth and status of the Church in Mexico during the colonial period.

parties, particularly in the 1980's. Anticlericalism is dying away. The literary and artistic revival that began in the 1920's has shown little sign of ending. The military is no longer a threat to internal stability and has been receiving a decreasing portion of the national budget since the era of Cárdenas. Mexico depends greatly upon tourism and the ability of many of its citizens to work in the United States. The harmony that existed in the early republic began to return when Mexico allied with the United States during World War II. No one doubts that the cultural and social influence of the United States has grown since the 1940's, but Mexican trends in eating, language, and heritage have also had an increasingly large impact upon the country, as evidenced by the growing Mexican-American community.

Douglas W. Richmond

Mexican Revolution

Three opponents of President Porfirio Díaz' regime are executed by firing squad in 1909, two years before revolution forced Díaz to flee Mexico for exile in Europe.

In May 1911, as Porfirio Díaz was leaving Mexico for exile in Paris after thirty-five years of dictatorial rule, he remarked that his successor, Francisco Madero, had unleashed a tiger. "Now let's see if he can control it," he said. Díaz' words proved prophetic; his ouster led to a bloody civil war that lasted a decade, cost the nation more than a million lives, and precipitated the first great revolution of the twentieth century.

DÍAZ' MEXICO

Díaz' astute understanding of Mexican society and politics explains how he was able to govern the nation from 1876 to 1911 (SEE Díaz Regime). Before Díaz' administration, Mexican politics had a well-deserved reputation for political instability. Since Mexico became a nation in 1821, the presidency had changed hands seventy-five times. Díaz had uncanny political instincts and knew how to play his opponents against one another. Governors were appointed, potentially ambitious military officers were shifted regularly to ensure they would not become too powerful, and journalists who criticized the regime often found themselves rotting in prison. His rule was never seriously questioned until 1910.

Díaz understood that Mexicans were tired of chronic political upheaval, and he focused much of his energy on promoting law and order and economic development. Díaz invested in the public infrastructure, especially railroads, ports, roads, and urban improvements; encouraged foreign investment; balanced the budget for the first time in Mexico's history; promoted the cultivation and production of export commodities such as silver, oil, copper, and fiber; and pacified the rural areas to spur economic development. Under his rule, regional elites and foreign investors took advantage of liberal

SUMMARY

➤ Rebels Francisco "Pancho" Villa and Emiliano Zapata helped Francisco Madero defeat Porfirio Díaz' regime in 1911.
➤ Zapata and his followers rebelled against Madero and were joined by Victoriano Huerta, who took over the country in 1913.
➤ Venustiano Carranza joined with Villa and lvaro Obregón in a counterrevolution and forced Huerta to resign in 1914.
➤ Carranza created a new constitution in 1917.
➤ Carranza was forced to flee in 1920 when Obregón revolted against him.

HOW REVOLUTIONARY WAS THE REVOLUTION?

Given how tumultuous the first ten years of fighting were, it is not surprising that historians have disagreed about how revolutionary the conflict was. Some argue that the revolution did overturn the old guard, the Díaz dictatorship, and replace it with a new revolutionary elite, made up for the most part of members of the middle class, who consolidated their hold on Mexican society in the 1920's and 1930's. This bourgeois elite forged a pact with peasants and workers and promoted a nationalistic revolution that reached its apogee during Lázaro Cárdenas' presidency from 1934 to 1940.

Revisionists have countered that the revolutionary regime bore a striking resemblance to the oligarchy that it had replaced, that many regional elites regained power after the fighting was over, and that the one-party state that evolved was just as antidemocratic, manipulative, and enamored of foreign investment as Díaz' dictatorship. To the extent that the revolution did create a welfare state for Mexico's underclasses, granting material improvements and a safety net, it succeeded, but political liberty still eludes Mexico's grasp.

Pancho Villa galloping alongside his column in 1914. Villa enjoyed the opportunities for personal glory created by the revolution and at one stage even allowed a Hollywood film crew to follow his progress. He afforded them suitable lighting conditions and advised them of the best angles for filming battle scenes.

land laws. Landownership became increasingly concentrated in fewer hands, often at the direct expense of indigenous communities who lost lands held for centuries. Peasants with few realistic options had little choice but to seek employment on the large landed estates, where they remained trapped through the mechanism of debt peonage.

THE RISE OF MADERO

Serious political opposition to Díaz' regime crystallized in the last five years of his rule. Activists such as Ricardo and Enrique Flores Magón founded the Mexican Liberal Party. They were harassed, jailed, and forced into exile. In 1908 two events encouraged opponents to become more outspoken. The aging Díaz, in an interview with American journalist Joel Creelman, intimated that he might not run again in 1910.

That same year, Francisco Madero published *La sucesión presidencial en 1910* (the presidential succession in 1910), which demanded that Díaz step down and not run in 1910. Madero formed a political party opposed to Díaz' reelection and campaigned throughout Mexico in 1909–1910 before he was jailed and driven into exile.

Convinced that Díaz would never relinquish power willingly, Madero, from exile in San Antonio, Texas, drafted his Plan of San Luis Potosí, which called for Mexicans to rise up in rebellion against the regime. Although Madero was interested primarily in political

Revolutionaries take over a locomotive at Cuernavaca, Morelos, south of Mexico City. The peasantry hoped to gain better and fairer living and working conditions from the revolution. They did so but only after a protracted political struggle in the two decades after the fighting had stopped.

reforms, Mexicans from all social classes responded to his call, and uprisings occurred along the northern frontier with the United States and just south of Mexico City in the state of Morelos in November 1910. Guerrilla leaders, including Pascual Orozco, Francisco "Pancho" Villa, and Emiliano Zapata, kept the federal troops off balance and won surprisingly easy victories. When Orozco and Villa captured Ciudad Juárez, the border city across the Rio Grande from El Paso in May 1911, Díaz decided to negotiate with the rebels. He quickly submitted his resignation on May 25 and went into exile.

Although Madero was the unquestioned leader of the Mexican Revolution, he decided to run for president in the fall 1911 elections to fulfill his commitment to democracy. While interim president Francisco León de la Barra ruled the nation, opponents of Madero—those who felt he represented a threat to the status quo and others who believed he was not committed to meaningful change—began to foment unrest. Zapata, a peasant leader from Morelos, demanded

that Madero make a commitment to restore lands lost during the dictatorship to the villages and indigenous communities.

Madero counseled patience to Zapata and his followers; lands would be returned under the law. Madero's tepid response to reform alienated former allies such as Zapata and Orozco, and his enemies mobilized to overthrow the president. Madero repeatedly had to call out the federal army to quash these rebellions.

HUERTA'S COUNTERREVOLUTION

General Victoriano Huerta, a Porfirian commander, succeeded in preserving Madero's presidency in the short run, but he became progressively more disenchanted with Madero. When a rebellion broke out in Mexico City in February 1913—an episode that came to be called the Ten Tragic Days— he switched his allegiance and sided with the rebels. Madero and his vice president, José María Pino Suárez, were imprisoned. Huerta signaled his decision to support the rebels when he signed an agreement entitled the

CAUSES AND EFFECTS

The Mexican Revolution was precipitated by thirty-five years of dictatorial rule by Porfirio Díaz. Opposition arose from disgruntled Mexicans who wanted democratic reforms, improved working conditions, and a return of village lands that had been lost during the dictatorship. Ten years of fighting left the country in shambles. While the country rebuilt in the 1920's, Mexican presidents gradually began to implement the provisions of the 1917 constitution.

Not until the presidency of Lázaro Cárdenas (1934–1940) would meaningful change come about.

PROFILE

FRANCISCO "PANCHO" VILLA (1878–1923)

Francisco "Pancho" Villa was a sharecropper on a hacienda from the northern state of Durango before the outbreak of hostilities in 1911. He became a bandit after clashing with his landlord and later joined Pascual Orozco's forces against Porfirio Díaz. Though he lacked a coherent social agenda, Villa was a charismatic leader who represented the interests of the cowboys and peasants of northern Mexico. After his crushing defeat at the Battle of Celaya in the spring of 1915, Villa was relegated to being a thorn in the side of Venustiano Carranza and the constitutionalists.

Villa was not only upset with his own desperate military predicament but also infuriated with U.S. president Woodrow Wilson, who recognized Carranza's government in October 1915. In January 1916 Villa's followers stopped a train carrying American mining engineers and technicians near Santa Isabel, Chihuahua, and murdered fifteen Americans. Two months later, Villa sent 485 men across the border to Columbus, New Mexico, burned the town to the ground, and killed eighteen Americans and wounded many more.

Americans were outraged, and Wilson responded by dispatching a small expedition led by General John J. Pershing. It took Pershing a week to get organized, and by that time, Villa had vanished into the northern Mexican desert. Six thousand U.S. troops wandered throughout northern Mexico, receiving little help from Mexicans. Carranza, concerned about this violation of Mexico's sovereignty, ordered Pershing to withdraw. The expedition finally left Mexico in January 1917. The United States spent $130 million in its futile attempt to punish the group. The raid sparked racism in the United States but swelled nationalistic pride in Mexico.

Pancho Villa (left) with General John J. Pershing, who carried out punitive raids against Villa in 1916. Pershing failed to catch Villa and so a commission was set up for Mexico and the United States to talk peace.

Pact of the Embassy, so named because final negotiations were completed in the U.S. embassy with the assistance of President William Howard Taft's ambassador, Henry Lane Wilson, who was convinced that Madero could no longer protect the property of U.S. companies in Mexico. Madero and Pino Suárez were assassinated under shadowy circumstances on February 21, 1913; contem-

porary observers believed that Huerta had murdered the two politicians.

When Huerta assumed power, many Mexicans were outraged that a new dictator had assumed power so soon after the overthrow of Díaz. A governor from the northeastern state of Coahuila, Venustiano Carranza, refused to recognize the new regime. Other northerners, Villa of Chihuahua and lvaro Obregón of Sonora, joined Carranza and signed the Plan of Guadalupe, which named Carranza first chief of the constitutionalist army. Zapata refused to support Huerta because he was convinced that the new dictator did not really intend to bring about agrarian reform. The United States government, now led by Woodrow Wilson, joined the constitutionalists in refusing to recognize Huerta. By the spring of 1914, Huerta's army was on the defensive, and Wilson, looking for a reason to intervene, found a pretext and ordered troops to land in the port of Veracruz. Huerta was forced to resign on July 8, 1914.

FORGING THE REVOLUTION

After Huerta's defeat, Carranza agreed that a convention should be held in Aguascalientes to determine who would be president until elections were held. The convention showed how bitterly divided the revolutionaries were. Zapata and Villa were convinced that Carranza was a political hack who had little interest in meaningful reform. In December 1914, Zapata and Villa met just outside of Mexico City and pledged their commitment to defeat the constitutionalists. Mexico once again plunged into civil war. As Zapata created havoc for constitutionalist forces in Morelos, Villa and his vaunted division of the north army fought the main constitutionalist armies in north central Mexico. In April 1915, at the Battle of Celaya, Villa was defeated by Carranza's chief general, Obregón. Villa would never again seriously threaten the constitutionalists. Although he and Zapata continued to launch hit-and-run raids, Carranza's leadership of the revolution was secured. Wilson, who had recalled the U.S. Marines after Huerta's ouster, officially recognized the first chief in October 1915.

Carranza, seeking some institutional legitimacy for his rule, convoked a constitutional convention in Querétaro in 1917. Although Carranza wanted to prevent a repeat of what happened in Aguascalientes, the debates in Querétaro were acrimonious. A group of radicals led by General Francisco Múgica pushed through a series of sweeping reforms. Among the most controversial articles in the new constitution were clauses that sought to weaken the influence of the Catholic Church; Article 127, which improved the rights of workers; and Article 27, which promised that lands seized illegally from the peasantry during Díaz' dictatorship would be restored and stated that the state had control over subsoil rights. This last clause upset foreign mining and oil companies, which worried that their investments would be jeopardized. Carranza accepted the constitution reluctantly and did little to enforce its provisions (SEE Mexican Constitution of 1917).

After Carranza won the presidency in special elections held in March 1917, he had difficulty pacifying the countryside. Villa was eventually bought off and given a large, landed estate. Carranza had Zapata ambushed and killed in 1919. Carranza's unwillingness to bring about change alienated some of his strongest allies. When Obregón launched a revolt in 1920, Carranza was forced to flee Mexico City and was shot. By 1920 the violent phase of the revolution had come to an end. Mexicans would have to rebuild their society in the wake of tremendous destruction and divisiveness.

Allen Wells

SEE ALSO:
CÁRDENAS GOVERNMENT; DÍAZ REGIME; MEXICAN CONSTITUTION OF 1917; MEXICAN MURALISTS; PARTIDO REVOLUCIONARIO INSTITUCIONAL; U.S.-MEXICAN RELATIONS.

FURTHER READING

•Benjamin, Thomas, and Mark Wasserman. *Provinces of the Revolution: Essays on Regional Mexican History, 1910–1929.* Albuquerque: University of New Mexico Press, 1990.

•Hart, John. *Revolutionary Mexico: The Coming and Process of the Mexican Revolution.* Berkeley: University of California Press, 1987.

•Katz, Friedrich. *The Secret War in Mexico: Europe, the United States and the Mexican Revolution.* Chicago: University of Chicago Press, 1981.

•Knight, Alan. *The Mexican Revolution.* 2 vols. New York: Cambridge University Press, 1986.

•Womack, John, Jr. *Zapata and the Mexican Revolution.* New York: Alfred A. Knopf, 1968.

Pancho Villa (center) sits in the president's chair in Mexico City on December 6, 1914. Emiliano Zapata sits on Villa's left. Both men would be assassinated: Zapata in 1919, Villa in 1923.

Mexican-Spanish Relations

General Franco, Spain's fascist leader, had close ties with Latin America after he took power in 1939. Mexico was almost alone in opposing him.

Mexico has always had a deeply split attitude toward Spain. Spain was venerated as the mother country, the source of Mexico's Hispanic culture, yet Mexicans often resented what they saw as Spain's colonial arrogance and condescension. By 1921 the Mexican Revolution had prevailed over the conservative rule customary within the country (SEE Mexican Revolution). Under leaders such as Plutarco Elías Calles and Lázaro Cárdenas, Mexican diplomacy tended to favor countries with socialist governments that disdained intervention by Western powers.

Although the authoritarian rule of Spain's dictator Miguel Primo de Rivera was overthrown in Spain in 1930, the republic that succeeded it faced harsh military opposition. This opposition became rebellion and then full-blown civil war by 1936.

Mexican president Cárdenas was sympathetic to Spain's legal government, the Spanish Republic. Backed by diplomatic advisers such as Isidro Fabela, the Cárdenas administration supplied food and arms to the Republican side and lobbied for its acceptance in the League of Nations and other worldwide forums. Mexico felt Republican Spain was an ideological ally, but in an effort to reassure Britain, France, and the U.S., Mexico's diplomatic efforts tended to stress the rebels' violation of international law. After the Republican government was forced to surrender to the rebels in 1939, Mexico took in many political refugees and became the seat for the Spanish government in exile.

Mexico was almost alone among Latin American countries in taking this position. Most other Latin American states felt ideological solidarity with the authoritarian regime of Francisco Franco, which controlled Spain after 1939. It was not until 1997 and the evolution of democratic government in Spain that Mexican-Spanish diplomatic relations were fully restored. The relationship between the countries was not as special as before, however. Mexico had become significantly closer to the U.S., as eventually evidenced by the North American Free Trade Agreement (SEE NAFTA), while Spain, though still interested in its former Latin American possessions, devoted most of its efforts to such European institutions as the North Atlantic Treaty Organization and the European Union.

Nicholas Birns

CAUSES AND EFFECTS

During the twentieth century, both Mexico and Spain had trouble establishing viable democracies, and their politics tended to swing between revolutionary upsurge and entrenched autocracy. Mexico and Spain shared a common language and heritage, but their relations were good only when like-minded governments were in power.

As the twenty-first century neared, Spain and Mexico were more anxious to integrate into the expanding global economy than to create a special role for each other. Spain's far greater wealth and stability meant that, for the moment, the mother country was the more important partner in the Spanish-Mexican diplomatic relationship.

SEE ALSO:
MEXICAN REVOLUTION; NAFTA; WORLD WAR II IN EUROPE.

Mexican War of Independence

By the beginning of the 1820's, much of the Mexican independence movement was suppressed. Two individuals, however, were continuing the fight: Guadalupe Victoria, who would later become the first president of the Mexican republic, and Vicente Guerrero, who was fighting in the mountains of southern Mexico. Augustín de Iturbide (1783–1824) was ordered to put down Guerrero's troops in the south.

Iturbide had resigned from the military but he had continued to maintain close contacts with Spanish authorities in both the church and state in Mexico and was reinstated partly because of the prominent people he knew. Iturbide's first task in defeating Guerrero and his forces was to establish contact with them. Iturbide established contact with Guerrero in February 1821 at Iguala, and decided to join forces with the rebel. The two men produced the Plan de Iguala, the plan that resulted in the independence of Mexico.

INDEPENDENCE SECURED

The Plan de Iguala appealed to both conservatives and the masses because of its call for independence. Equally important, Victoria supported it. By 1821, Spain had appointed a new viceroy in Mexico, Juan O'Donojú. The new viceroy negotiated with Iturbide and agreed to accept the Plan de Iguala. Iturbide's army marched into Mexico City in triumph, and a provisional government was created. Mexico became independent eleven years after Miguel Hidalgo y Costilla's famous proclamation, El Grito de Dolores.

The provisional Mexican government knew that the country needed to have international recognition and legitimacy to function effectively as an independent nation. Many conservatives wanted to create a monarchy. Iturbide, realizing that he did not have enough support to take over the nation himself, decided to stage a spontaneous demonstration for himself with help from his troops. This attracted a large crowd, which shouted "Long live Agustín I, Emperor of Mexico, long live the Emperor!" After

General Guadalupe Victoria was elected the first president of Mexico when Mexico was declared a republic two years after the end of the War of Independence.

that, Congress named Iturbide constitutional emperor of Mexico, and he was officially crowned in the summer of 1822.

THE MEXICAN EMPIRE

Iturbide appointed an interim congress to get Mexico's political house in order. Iturbide's government included many wealthy individuals and those who belonged to the Mexican aristocracy. Former independence leaders like Guerrero and Victoria were left out of decision making.

The Mexican monarchy, which lasted less than a year, had the monumental task of mending the economic and political problems facing the empire. The wars of

SUMMARY

➤ In the 1820's, Augustín de Iturbide joined with rebel Vicente Guerrero and declared Mexico's independence from Spain.
➤ Iturbide became constitutional emperor of Mexico in 1822 but was unable to solve the country's political and economic problems.
➤ In 1822, Antonio López de Santa Anna led a revolt against Iturbide.
➤ Iturbide abdicated his throne in 1823 and fled to exile in Europe.
➤ Iturbide returned from exile and was executed in July 1823.

Agustín de Iturbide was crowned emperor of Mexico in 1822.

been severely affected by over a decade of war. Moreover, because of the Napoleonic wars and the Mexican War of Independence, commerce to and from Mexico had been reduced. Iturbide had little money or revenue and had a difficult time borrowing and securing loans. The monarchy, moreover, had to keep paying the army, which was the core of its support. In the end, Iturbide had to extract loans from the people of Mexico and confiscate property. His popularity diminished. Iturbide soon dissolved congress.

THE FALL OF ITURBIDE

The monarchy was criticized because of its ill-conceived plans to rejuvenate the nation, and plots against Iturbide began to unfold. In December 1822 the commander of Veracruz, Antonio López de Santa Anna, along with his troops, roamed the streets of Veracruz, proclaiming a republic. Santa Anna's revolt, the Plan of Veracruz, quickly gained support, including that of Guerrero and Victoria.

Iturbide ordered José Antonio Echávarri, the captain general of Veracruz, to defeat Santa Anna. Echávarri, however, much as Iturbide had done a few years earlier, switched allegiances and sided with Santa Anna. The rebels began moving toward Mexico City, taking control of the provinces along the way. Iturbide realized that support for his monarchy was seriously undermined. He abdicated his throne in March 1823 and went into exile in Europe.

ITURBIDE'S RETURN FROM EXILE

Iturbide returned to Mexico from exile in mid-1823, proclaiming that he came back to

independence had disrupted Mexican agriculture and mining. Mexico's wealth and profit lay in its gold and silver mines in the central part of the country, and this area had

CAUSES AND EFFECTS

The causes of the Mexican insurrection were both social and political. The *criollos* (full-blooded Spaniards born in the New World) and mestizos (people of both Spanish and Indian ancestry) in Mexico and elsewhere in the Americas were discriminated against. The *criollos* and mestizos, who were one social strata below the *criollos*, were prohibited from climbing the social ladder and could not aspire to prominent political and religious office. Only Spaniards born in Spain could hold high positions in the Church and state in Mexico and the rest of the Americas. The Mexican movement for independence brought an end to the existence of the Spanish political, social, and economic system in Mexico.

By 1822, independence was secured and culminated in the short-lived Mexican empire under Augustín de Iturbide. Independence did not provide answers but instead raised questions on issues surrounding nation building. By 1823, Iturbide was out of power, and, as a consequence, new socioeconomic elements arose in Mexico. The *criollo* middle class came into power. After the fall of Iturbide's empire, the Mexican people clamored for a new government centered around a republic.

LAWS AND CASES

PLAN DE IGUALA

The Plan de Iguala was a simple agreement. Augustín de Iturbide and Vicente Guerrero would join forces and bring about Mexican independence. They would then establish a junta to rule for Ferdinand VII, the king of Spain, who had been deposed and forced by Spanish liberals in 1820 to accept the liberal Spanish constitution of 1812. In effect, Mexico was to be a constitutional monarchy under Ferdinand VII. The Plan de Iguala was a fervently nationalistic independence manifesto. It called for a peaceful transfer of power. With viceroyal Juan O'Donojú's acceptance of the manifesto, Iturbide succeeded in bringing about the long-awaited independence of Mexico.

The Plan de Iguala called for three guarantees to be given to the Mexican people: independence, religion, and the elimination of legal barriers intruding upon the freedom of the people. *Criollos* wanted equality with Spaniards born in Spain. Iturbide and Guerrero's army would hence be known as the Army of the Three Guarantees. The three colors of their army's flag represented their three promises to the Mexican people.

Ferdinand VII, the deposed king of Spain, on whose behalf Vicente Guerrero and Augustín de Iturbide intended to rule Mexico following the War of Independence.

SEE ALSO:
MESTIZOS, METIS & MULATTOES; MEXICAN REPUBLIC; MEXICAN-SPANISH RELATIONS; MEXICAN WAR OF INDEPENDENCE.

FURTHER READING
•Bazant, Jan. *A Concise History of Mexico from Hidalgo to Cardenas, 1805–1940.* Cambridge, England: Cambridge University Press, 1977.
•Caruso, John Anthony. *The Liberators of Mexico.* New York: Pageant Press, 1954.
•De Lara, L. Gutierrez, and Edgcumb Pinchon. *The Mexican People: Their Struggle for Freedom.* New York: Arno Press, 1970.
•Robertson, William Spencer. *Iturbide of Mexico.* Durham, N.C.: Duke University Press, 1952.

the Americas to preserve the liberty of Mexico and to save the area from anarchy and ruin. The Mexican congress had earlier declared that if Iturbide ever set foot again on Mexican soil, he was to be considered both an enemy of Mexico and a traitor to his country. As a result, when Iturbide did return to Mexico, he was captured and sentenced to death.

In July 1823 Iturbide met his death in front of a firing squad. He died claiming that he was not a traitor to his country but a Mexican with honor.

David Trevino

795

Miami Riots

National Guardsmen on patrol during the Miami Riots in May 1980. Sixteen people died in the riots following the acquittal of five police officers for the killing of Arthur Lee McDuffie, an African-American.

CAUSES AND EFFECTS

African-Americans in Miami were frustrated with a justice system that they saw as biased against them. Many claimed that cases of police brutality against them had gone unpunished. African-Americans were also disturbed by the apparent economic success of Cubans, which, some blacks believed, was achieved at their expense. When, on May 17, 1980, an all-white jury acquitted five police officers of killing a black man during a routine traffic stop, rioting and violence ensued. The rioting resulted in sixteen deaths, caused 400 injuries, and wreaked an estimated $100 million in property damage.

SEE ALSO:
CIVIL RIGHTS
MOVEMENT; CUBAN
REVOLUTION; DETROIT
RIOTS; LOS ANGELES
RIOTS; MARIEL BOAT
LIFT; RACE RIOTS OF
1943; WATTS RIOT.

On December 17, 1979, Miami police attempted to stop Arthur Lee McDuffie, a thirty-three-year-old African-American manager with a life insurance company, who was speeding on a motorcycle. McDuffie, who had lost his license for paying a previous traffic fine with a bad check, attempted to flee from the police and led them on a chase. In the end, a badly beaten McDuffie was admitted to a hospital, where he died. The police claimed that he had been injured while resisting arrest, but five police officers were brought to trial. In exchange for immunity, two other officers testified against them. These two officers said that McDuffie was giving himself up when the enraged officers attacked him.

On May 17, 1980, an all-white jury acquitted the five Miami police officers on the grounds that it could not be determined who had killed McDuffie. Word of the acquittal spread through Miami. A protest rally in front of the justice building began to turn violent.

A crowd gathered in Liberty City, a large black neighborhood, chanting "McDuffie! McDuffie!" The fury of the crowd intensified and turned against whites in general. The people began hunting down any whites they could find, brutally beating and stabbing them. A number of African-American men and women stood up to the mobs and managed to save the lives of several whites.

Attacks against whites gradually lessened in number, and the rioters turned their attention to looting stores and firebombing. Cuban-owned businesses were targeted because of the tension between African-Americans and economically successful Cubans. The police closed off a 250-block area and imposed a curfew around it. Firefighters were not allowed into the closed territory because of snipers, and many buildings burned to the ground.

Some Miami police officers began to respond with their own lawlessness, vandalizing cars left in the parking lots of looted stores and painting the words "thief" or "looter" on them. An uneasy peace was finally imposed on May 19, when Florida governor Bob Graham sent thirty-eight hundred National Guardsmen into the riot-torn neighborhood.

Carl L. Bankston III

Military Draft

During the Civil War many financial inducements were offered as a means of recruiting men for military service. In the twentieth century there was a large-scale, organized army draft in the United States for both world wars.

During the Civil War, volunteerism proved to be an inadequate means of fulfilling the manpower needs of the Union and Confederate armies. The Confederacy began using conscription statutes, and the Union followed its example, realizing that volunteer forces needed ample compensation and relied on an emotional involvement with the war.

On March 3, 1863, President Abraham Lincoln signed the Enrollment Act, the first national conscription legislation. The law mandated all able-bodied male citizens between the ages of twenty and forty-five to fulfill a military service if called on by the president. Initial enrollment was much slower than anticipated because of statutory exemptions, which included federal government employees, preachers (among other professions), and anyone deemed physically, mentally, or morally unfit for service.

The law was written in such a way that draftees could purchase a replacement or pay a "commutation fee" of $300 to avoid service altogether. Working-class citizens found the deferments unfair; thus the Civil War has often been called "a rich man's war and a poor man's fight" (SEE Civil War). President Lincoln did not send the law for judicial ruling, fearing that a national conscription would be found unconstitutional. Although only 46,000 of the 2.1 million Union troops were draftees and 118,000 were substitutes, critics of the draft argued that the Union used conscription to gain large numbers of men to win the war over the Confederacy.

THE EFFECTS OF INDUSTRIALIZATION

By the end of the nineteenth century, many of the world's leading nations had developed nationally trained militias with a mass

SUMMARY

➤ In 1863, President Abraham Lincoln created the first national draft legislation to raise Union forces during the Civil War.
➤ In 1917, the Selective Service System was created to establish a comprehensive draft system.
➤ During the Vietnam War, the large number of conscripts made it difficult for the army to train and process them adequately.
➤ In response to opposition to the draft, President Richard Nixon instituted a lottery system to replace the old draft, then in 1973 created an all-volunteer army.

Drafted men report for service at Camp Travis, San Antonio, Texas, after the United States had entered World War I.

conscripted reserve, but the United States was late to follow suit.

Beginning in 1915, the United States experienced a "preparedness movement." National slogans and propaganda were used to persuade people that a national draft was a more economically feasible way to raise troops for war. The voluntary enlistment program had become costly and outdated. American citizens became convinced that the United States should create a mass army of citizen reservists.

In April 1917 the Selective Service System was developed to establish a comprehensive draft system. It allowed the United States to increase its national reserve to be effective against other world powers. During World War I (SEE World War I & the U.S.), the Selective Service System drafted 2.8 million men ages eighteen to twenty-five: 72 percent of the army war troops. There was

virtually no opposition to the Selective Service System, and in 1918 the U.S. Supreme Court ruled that national conscription was constitutional.

During World War II (SEE World War II in Europe; World War II in the Pacific), the draft laws went through several revisions. Before the war, the ages were twenty-one to thirty-five, and draftees were obligated to serve for only one year. In 1941, however, Congress narrowly voted to extend the draftees' service time. Later, the law was again expanded to include men eighteen through thirty-eight and required them to serve through the end of the war. The draft did not end, however, with the war. Despite efforts in 1947 by President Harry S. Truman to reduce the draft and rely more on volunteerism, by 1948 the draft legislation was again in effect (SEE Executive Order 8802; Truman's Presidency).

DRAFT NUMBERS INCREASE

By 1953, approximately 1.5 million men (ages eighteen to twenty-five) had been drafted for the Korean War (SEE Korean War). The large numbers of conscripts in Korea (and again in Vietnam) made it difficult to train the troops adequately. The Vietnam War in the mid- to late 1960's had the largest percentages of conscripted men. By 1969, 89 percent of the soldiers and over half of the casualties in Vietnam were draftees. The abundance of draftees forced a high rotation, making it difficult for troops to adapt. The results were disastrous and caused a national outrage toward the U.S. military (SEE Vietnam War). In 1968, Richard M. Nixon, in his presidential campaign, vowed to eliminate the draft. As president, he began by firing Major General Lewis B. Hershey, who had been in charge of the draft since

CAUSES AND EFFECTS

Several states in the United States enacted conscription laws for wars such as the American Revolution and the War of 1812, but a national conscription was considered oppressive and undemocratic. With the Civil War, massive casualties, disease, irregular pay, and the duration of the war created a manpower shortage that forced the Union to consider conscription. Initially, the creation of a national conscription law for the United States was largely opposed. Nonetheless, the draft was fundamental in making the United States a world military leader after World War I. Also, the controversy over the draft was a factor in increasing volunteerism until the United States could sustain an all-volunteer force.

VIEWPOINTS

CONSCIENTIOUS OBJECTION AND ANTIWAR PROTESTS

The call for the first draftees in 1863 caused thousands to actively resist the draft and violent riots broke out immediately in New York City. Opponents claimed the draft was not fair to men who were unable to pay substitutes and commutation fees. In an amendment to the draft in 1864, men opposed to the war for religious reasons could receive deferment from battle on the grounds of conscientious objection.

During World War I, support for the draft increased, and few antidraft demonstrations occurred. Protest was asserted through political debate, evasion, and illegal refusal to register. Of the thousands who claimed conscientious objection, many were given civilian jobs, others had their claims denied, and some were imprisoned.

During the Vietnam War, the Supreme Court ruled that registrants could claim conscientious objection for moral or ethical reasons. Men could also receive deferment through other loopholes. Consequently, draftees during the Vietnam War were primarily working-class and minority youths. African-Americans, for example, made up 11 percent of the U.S. population but 15 percent of the army's war deaths. Antidraft sentiment escalated during the Vietnam War, and riots, draft card burnings, sit-ins, and other demonstrations occurred nationwide.

SEE ALSO:
CIVIL WAR; EXECUTIVE ORDER 8802; KOREAN WAR; PEACE MOVEMENT; PERSIAN GULF WAR; TRUMAN'S PRESIDENCY; VIETNAM WAR; WORLD WAR I & THE U.S.; WORLD WAR II IN EUROPE; WORLD WAR II IN THE PACIFIC.

FURTHER READING
•Chambers, John Whiteclay, II. *To Raise an Army*. New York: Free Press, 1987.
•Cohen, Eliot A. *Citizens and Soldiers*. Ithaca, N.Y.: Cornell University Press, 1985.

World War II. In 1970, President Nixon instituted a random selection "lottery" for calling young men and hired a staff to explore the options of an all-volunteer army.

In 1973, the All Volunteer Force (AVF) was established to decrease the need for conscription. The government offered better wages and benefits to entice people to enlist. After a cease-fire ending the Vietnam War in 1973, no more Americans were drafted. In the late 1970's, Congress increased volunteerism when it made the military more attractive by raising wages and providing education benefits.

After increasing testing standards for new recruits, the United States was able to effectively train an all-volunteer army. In 1991, the Persian Gulf War was the first American-involved conflict to use an all-volunteer army since the first draft laws were created (SEE Persian Gulf War). The high numbers of existing troops and the time needed to train new recruits made it unnecessary for the United States to revitalize the draft.

Caralee Hutchinson

President Richard Nixon visits the 1st Infantry Division of the U.S. Army in Vietnam in July 1969. Some young Americans evaded service in Vietnam by fleeing to non-aligned countries such as Canada and Sweden.

Million Man March

Louis Farrakhan organized the Million Man March of African-Americans in October 1995.

CAUSES AND EFFECTS

During the 1990's, public concern with crime and an increase in white supremacist groups heightened tensions between the races. The acquittal of four Los Angeles police officers in April 1992 for beating a black man who had resisted arrest ignited two days of rioting, looting, and citywide fires in Los Angeles.

Then, on October 3, 1995, a not-guilty verdict in the trial of former football player O. J. Simpson for the murder of his wife, a white woman, and a visitor, also white, accentuated what analysts saw as a widening divide between whites and African-Americans. A predominantly black jury had rendered the verdict, and opinions of its validity appeared to be split along racial lines.

Occurring at the height of the media storm surrounding the Simpson trial, the Million Man March forced Americans to move beyond racial stereotypes and acknowledge African-Americans as caring, responsible individuals.

SEE ALSO:
CIVIL RIGHTS
MOVEMENT; LOS
ANGELES RIOTS;
MALCOLM X'S
ASSASSINATION.

On October 16, 1995, more than 800,000 African-Americans, primarily men, participated in the Rights and Responsibilities Rally in Washington, D.C., known as the Million Man March. The demonstration was organized by Nation of Islam leader Louis Farrakhan and directed by the former head of the National Association for the Advancement of Colored People (NAACP) Benjamin F. Chavis, Jr.

In his keynote speech, "Toward a More Perfect Union," Farrakhan encouraged his audience, particularly the men to whom the day was devoted, to engage themselves fully in the spiritual leadership of their communities and families. The Reverend Jesse Jackson, founder of the National Rainbow Coalition, the Reverend Al Sharpton of New York City, Bishop H. H. Brookins of the African Methodist Episcopal (AME) Church, president of the Southern Christian Leadership Conference Joseph Lowery, noted poet Maya Angelou, civil-rights activist Rosa Parks, Malcolm X's widow Betty Shabazz, Washington mayor Marion Barry, Baltimore mayor Kurt Schmoke, Detroit mayor Dennis Archer, and child evangelist Ayinde Jean-Baptiste were among the many who spoke.

Jean-Baptiste, twelve years old, encouraged African-American fathers to deepen their involvement with their children.

Controversy had surrounded the event, some denouncing Farrakhan as having initiated the rally to ameliorate his racist image (he had previously made anti-Semitic and other inflammatory remarks). The NAACP, headed by Myrlie Evers-Williams, would not endorse the rally.

Organizers criticized the media for its lack of coverage leading up to the rally (word was spread primarily though black radio) and the National Park Service for its low estimate of the number of participants (about 400,000). Feminists claimed their interests had been ignored, objecting to the focus on black men and their roles.

Nevertheless, the speeches' unifying themes and the peaceful atmosphere of the televised gathering impressed the nation at large: African-Americans' own "silent majority" had stood up *en masse* to counter a racist image of their young men as criminals and to acknowledge their responsibility, and their power, to improve life in their own communities and to bridge racial divides.

Chris Moose

Missions of the Spanish Friars

As a result of the explorations launched by Juan Ponce de León in 1513 and Francisco Vásquez de Coronado in 1540, Spain colonized vast regions of North America. To maintain control of these territories, Spain built military garrisons, or presidios, in New Spain (present-day Mexico and Central America) and authorized and encouraged the Catholic Church to establish missionary settlements along the frontiers where foreign invasion was most likely.

Though soldiers and statesmen established the presidios, Jesuit and Franciscan missionaries founded the missions with the aim of converting Native Americans to Christianity. Missionaries entered the vast uncharted wilderness of North America and sought out Native American communities to convert. They quickly taught the Native Americans in the ways of the Church and Spanish empire.

The Mission San Diego de Alcalá, established in 1769, houses California's first church. The mission was built by Father Junípero Serra, a Spanish friar.

Early in the sixteenth century, Franciscan missionaries established missions in present-day Florida. Some forty missions were founded, but virtually every mission was laid waste by French and British incursions, European disease, and indigenous rebellions. By 1706, the English had destroyed the last of the missions. Unlike the Florida missions, many of those in New Mexico, Arizona, Texas, and Upper California fared significantly better. Some survived to form the basis of twentieth-century church parishes and communities.

The missions and colonies of New Mexico, established at the beginning of the seventeenth century, were constructed at the

SUMMARY

➤ Spain encouraged Jesuits and Franciscans to establish missionary communities in North America so that it could maintain control over its colonies.

➤ Forty missions were established in present-day Florida in the early 1500's, but by 1706 none remained.

➤ Mission communities were also founded in present-day New Mexico and Texas.

➤ Jesuit missionary Eusebio Francisco Kino established missions in present-day Arizona and Sonora.

➤ Franciscan friar Junípero Serra founded the first nine of twenty-one missions established in Upper California between 1769 and 1823.

Between the seventeenth and nineteenth centuries, missionary settlements sprang up across present-day California, Arizona, and Sonora, which were part of the Spanish empire. Franciscan and Jesuit missionaries had come to New Spain with the aim of converting Indians to Roman Catholicism.

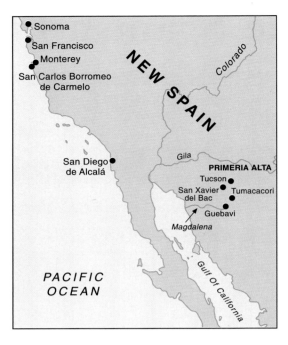

FURTHER READING
•Bannon, John Francis, ed. *Bolton and the Spanish Borderlands.* Norman: University of Oklahoma Press, 1964.
•Faulk, Odie B., and Laura E. Faulk. *Defenders of the Interior Provinces: Presidial Soldiers on the Northern Frontier of New Spain.* Albuquerque: Albuquerque Museum of History, 1988.
•Jackson, Robert H., and Edward Castillo. *Indians, Franciscans, and Spanish Colonization: The Impact of the Mission System on California Indians.* Albuquerque: University of New Mexico Press, 1995.
(Continued on page 803)

heart of preexisting brick and sandstone Indian pueblos, but the missions in Texas, established in the early to mid-eighteenth century, were designed to protect against Apache raids and French incursions from the north and the east. The six surviving missions look like garrisons or walled towns, complete with defensive perimeters, towers, and gun ports.

The Arizona and Sonora territories, known as Primeria Alta, were initially colonized by the Jesuit missionary Eusebio Francisco Kino. By 1695, Father Kino had established a chain of missions along the Altar and Magdalena Rivers and another chain of missions in Mexico near Dolores, Sonora. By 1700, he had founded the mission communities of San Xavier del Bac near Tucson, Arizona, and Tumacacori and Guebavi in southern Arizona. Historian Herbert Eugene Bolton has said that Kino's explorations were essentially the work of an itinerant missionary.

Kino devoted much time to teaching and baptizing the Indians whom he encountered. Kino introduced the arts of stock raising, ranching, and farming and European-style architecture and settlement into each mission community that he founded. The Franciscans who followed Kino into this area in the late eighteenth century owe much to this tireless, black-robed Jesuit missionary, explorer, cartographer, architect, rancher, and farmer.

The first missions of Upper California were founded by Franciscan friar Junípero Serra. The viceroy of New Spain, Carlos Francisco de Croix, and the *visitador general* of King Charles III, José de Gálvez, ordered Gaspar de Portolá, the governor of California, and Serra to colonize Upper California to fully claim the region for the Spanish empire.

Serra founded the settlements of San Diego de Alcalá in the south in 1769 and San Carlos Borromeo de Carmelo in the north in 1770. According to Bolton's 1927 account, Portolá and Serra were ordered to "establish garrisons at San Diego and Monterey and to plant missions, under military protection, to convert and civilize the natives." Serra founded the first nine of twenty-one missions established in Upper California between 1769 and 1823.

Franciscan and Jesuit missionaries, in their zeal to convert the Indians to Christianity and christen them citizens of the

CAUSES AND EFFECTS

Since the earliest colonial explorations in 1542, the Spanish clergy sought permission and support to colonize Upper California and convert the native inhabitants to Christianity. Such requests went largely unheeded until the mid-eighteenth century, when Russian fur traders explored the northern coast of Upper California and established colonies there, threatening Spain's largely uncontested claims to the territory. Under orders of the king of Spain, a colonial expedition consisting of soldiers, traders, and priests set out to establish a chain of missions and settlements along the coast of Upper California, from San Diego (1769) northward to Monterey and eventually Sonoma. Over the next fifty years, twenty-one missions were established in the area. As a result, Russian expansion was halted, and Spanish political and military control was consolidated after nearly two centuries of neglect.

PROFILE

JUNÍPERO SERRA

In July 1769 Franciscan friar Junípero Serra founded the first of Upper California's twenty-one Spanish missions on a hillside overlooking San Diego Bay. For the next fifteen years, Serra supervised the establishment of a chain of missions that extended as far north as San Francisco and converted nearly seventeen thousand Indians to Christianity. Driven by a passionate desire to spread the Christian faith, Serra worked tirelessly to establish these missions despite the lack of necessary supplies, the devastating impact of European diseases on the Indians, and personal illness. By 1782, Serra had established nine missions, each not only a religious center but also a base from which Spain could further its economic and political expansion.

Through his missionary work, Serra introduced European and Christian doctrines and customs to thousands of Indians. In addition, because each mission was required to be self-sufficient, the Indians who became mission community residents were introduced to farming, ranching, carpentry, tanning, candle making, and ironwork.

These skills led to the prosperity and productivity of the mission communities and the economic development of Upper California. Because, however, of the vast cultural and biological differences between the Indians and the Spaniards, by the mid-1800's, only a few of the mission Indians survived the onslaught of disease and the enforced disruption of their traditional lifestyle.

The room in which Junípero Serra lived in the Carmel Mission in Carmel, California.

SEE ALSO: CORONADO'S EXPEDITION; DE SOTO'S EXPEDITION; OÑATE'S NEW MEXICO EXPEDITION; PUEBLO REVOLT; SPANISH COLONIAL POLICIES; SPANISH CONQUEST.

FURTHER READING
•Kennedy, Roger G. *Mission: The History and Architecture of the Missions of North America.* Edited and designed by David Larkin with photography by Michael Freeman. New York: Houghton Mifflin, 1993.
•Kessell, John L. *Kiva, Cross, and Crown: The Pecos Indians and New Mexico, 1540–1840.* Washington, D.C.: National Park Service and the U.S. Department of the Interior, 1979.
•Mendoza, Rubén G., and Cruz C. Torres. "Hispanic Traditional Technology and Material Culture in the United States." In *Handbook of Hispanic Cultures in the United States: Anthropology,* edited and introduced by Thomas Weaver. Houston, Tex.: Arte Público Press and the Instituto de Cooperación Iberoamericana, 1994.
•Morgado, Martin J. *Junípero Serra: A Pictorial Biography.* Monterey, Calif.: Siempre Adelante Publishing, 1991.
•Wakely, David. *A Sense of Mission: Historic Churches of the Southwest.* San Francisco: Chronicle Books, 1994.

Spanish empire, explored, charted, and colonized vast regions and founded hundreds of colonial settlements. Though many of the mission communities of the late eighteenth century did not survive the internal turmoil, enforced secularization, and foreign intrusions of that time, many major American cities owe their origins to these early Spanish colonial and indigenous communities.

Ruben G. Mendoza and Kenneth Halla

Mississippi Valley Exploration

Jacques Marquette, a French missionary, undertook extensive explorations in the Mississippi Valley during the seventeenth century.

SUMMARY

➤ French Canada sought control of the Mississippi River Valley to expand the lucrative fur trade.
➤ In 1673 Jacques Marquette and Louis Jolliet traveled partway down the Mississippi but lost all their maps and journals.
➤ In 1682 René Robert Cavelier, sieur de La Salle, followed the Mississippi to the Gulf of Mexico and claimed the whole Mississippi Valley for France, naming it Louisiana.
➤ Battles with the Fox tribe and opposition from the Jesuits and Louis XIV further hampered expansion efforts.
➤France was unable to settle the Mississippi Valley and surrendered the area to Britain in 1763.

On May 17, 1673, the Jesuit missionary Jacques Marquette and the explorer Louis Jolliet set out from Montreal, Canda, with five other men and two canoes in search of the "great water" in the west. Louis de Buade, comte de Frontenac and governor of French Canada, sent them in hopes of expanding French control of the fur trade within the region.

The twenty-seven-year-old Jolliet, born in Canada, had studied for the priesthood, but while still a student, he had discovered that he was more interested in adventure and music. By the time he joined the 1673 expedition, Jolliet had made several canoe trips into the northern Great Lakes region and had gained a reputation for bravery and high-quality maps. On one of his journeys into Lake Superior, he had been told by Indians of a great river to the south that

eventually flowed into a southern sea (the Gulf of Mexico). Marquette, who was born and educated in France, had arrived in Canada in 1666. He dedicated his life to the service of his fellow men and was especially interested in bringing the Christian message to Indians. In 1671 he built his first mission church in St. Ignace in the upper peninsula of present-day Michigan.

THE EXPEDITION OF MARQUETTE AND JOLLIET

By late May, the expedition reached Green Bay, where Indians warned them that farther south were horrible monsters and "people without mercy" who would certainly kill their whole party if they continued their journey. They also said that there was such terrible heat in the direction the expedition was headed that people could burn to death merely from the sun's rays. The explorers continued their journey despite these warnings. On June 17, after canoeing down the Wisconsin River for several days, Jolliet and Marquette reached the Mississippi. They continued down the river for several weeks until they reached the Arkansas River. Indians told them they were within three days of another white settlement, probably a small Spanish outpost on the Gulf of Mexico. The Frenchmen decided to turn back rather than risk being taken prisoners by their major rivals in the New World.

On the return trip the two canoes and seven men decided to head up the Illinois River rather than go all the way back to the Wisconsin River. Guided by Indians, they eventually made it to the southern tip of Lake Michigan through the "Chicago" portage, a swampy marsh that was too shallow even for canoes, forcing them to carry their boats the last several miles to the shore. At the point where the tiny Chicago River entered Lake Michigan, they found an Indian village. Marquette promised to return to the village after delivering his report on his explorations to the French governor. On the return trip to Montreal, tragedy struck, however, and Jolliet's canoe capsized in a storm, losing all the maps and journals the explorers had kept.

Jolliet made it back to Montreal and tried to redraw his maps from memory but was not very successful. Marquette eventually kept his promise, returning to the village late in 1674. He built a mission and a small shelter for the winter. The bitter cold destroyed his health, and he tried to return to Green Bay the next summer but never made it. He died on May 18 and was buried in the wilderness. The exploration of the Mississippi Valley ended in disaster.

FRONTENAC AND FUR TRADING

Frontenac continued to show interest in expanding the French fur-trading empire into the Great Lakes region and the Mississippi Valley (SEE French Colonial Policies). Furs were the major source of wealth in French Canada, and there continued to be a huge market for animal skins in Europe. Fur trappers generally acquired the furs directly from Indians and brought them in huge quantities to Montreal. The numbers of animals in older regions of French Canada, mainly Quebec, were dwindling, however, making expansion necessary.

Frontenac had run into opposition to his plans for an expanded empire, chiefly from Catholic missionaries who wanted the Mississippi region to be turned into a giant Indian reserve. Here Indians and missionaries would live in peace and harmony, free from the corrupting influence of business and profit making. The priests wanted to ban brandy and rum and prohibit fur trapping.

The king of France, Louis XIV, was heavily influenced by his Catholic advisers and he also blamed fur trappers for a very costly war with the Iroquois, France's chief rival for furs in the region. The Iroquois had

King Louis XIV of France, known as the Sun King, issued a ban on fur trapping in the Mississippi Valley in 1676. This restricted French explorations in the valley.

CAUSES AND EFFECTS

France had controlled the northern Great Lakes from its settlement at Montreal (New France) since 1610. It wanted to expand the fur trade, a source of great wealth for French merchants, by expanding south into the Mississippi River Valley. Some officials even began thinking about establishing a water route from New France to the Gulf of Mexico.

The French explored the valley all the way to the gulf and gained control of the fur trade after a series of wars with the Fox tribe. They failed, however, to build successful permanent settlements, and attempts to establish agricultural communities failed.

tried to buy all furs trapped by Indians in the northwest and sell them to British agents in New York. Louis XIV decided to turn control of the region and the Indians over to the Jesuits and issued a ban on all fur trapping in the Mississippi Valley in 1676. This ban proved impossible to enforce and it was quickly abandoned. Wars and conflict with the Iroquois continued (SEE Iroquois Confederacy).

LA SALLE'S EXPEDITIONS

In 1679, René Robert Cavelier, sieur de La Salle (SEE Cartier & Roberval Expeditions), began his attempt to bring the water route linking the Great Lakes and Montreal with the Gulf of Mexico entirely under French control. La Salle built several forts in the Mississippi Valley, including one at Peoria and another at Ottawa along the Illinois

Marquette and Jolliet
1. St Ignace church built by Marquette in 1671
2. Green Bay
3. Limit of 1673 exploration
4. "Chicago" portage

In 1673 Jacques Marquette and Louis Jolliet began an expedition into the wilderness, part of which saw them canoe down the Mississippi River.

River. In 1682 he led an expedition as far south as the Gulf of Mexico and claimed the Mississippi Valley for France, naming it Louisiana. In 1684, La Salle set sail from France for the Gulf Coast with four ships and more than two hundred colonists.

Unable to find the mouth of the river, La Salle landed instead in Texas. After three years of wandering in the wilderness in Texas and Arkansas and undergoing extreme hardship and hunger, La Salle's group revolted and killed their leader.

THE "INDIAN MENACE"

The French control of the Mississippi Valley depended on good relations with the Indians. Only the Fox did not get along well with French traders in the area, and they openly aligned with the invading Iroquois. In 1712 the Fox Wars began, a series of battles that would continue for almost fifty years. The Fox reacted violently after the French signed an alliance with the Lakota Sioux, the Fox's ancient enemy to the west. After the death of Louis XIV in 1715, the French government decided to repeal the ban on fur trading and expanded the war against the Fox. In 1720 a French force destroyed a Fox village, killing more than 300 warriors, women, and children. The remaining Fox escaped to Wisconsin, and the hostilities seemed to be over (SEE Fox Wars).

With the "Indian menace" now gone, the Mississippi Valley appeared more ready for permanent settlements. The government in Paris established the Company of the West, also known as the Mississippi Company, to recruit settlers. The entire Mississippi Valley was incorporated into the Louisiana Territory (SEE Louisiana Purchase), and the company was given a monopoly on the fur trade and also on the newly discovered iron mines in Illinois and Missouri.

Under its contract, six thousand whites and three thousand black slaves were to be imported into the territory. Few Frenchmen wanted to emigrate, however, even when offered free land. The Company of the West resorted to kidnapping prisoners, homeless people, and abandoned children living in the streets of Paris. They were marched in chains onto ships, but many died en route to the

PROFILE

SIEUR DE LA SALLE (1643–1687)

René Robert Cavelier, sieur de La Salle, was born to a family of wealthy merchants in Rouen, France. He attended religious school and hoped to become a missionary. He had difficulty conforming to the rules of a seminary, however, and soon dropped out.

At age twenty-four he crossed the Atlantic to New France. He dreamed of finding a water passage to China and made several attempts to achieve that goal, eventually getting as far west as Lake Superior. Indians talked him into abandoning this project and advised him to find the "great river" to the south, which they assured him would eventually lead to a vast southern sea. In 1682 he set out with his friend Henri Tonti to explore the entire length of the Mississippi River.

The expedition reached the Gulf of Mexico in April and claimed the entire valley for the king of France, Louis XIV, naming it Louisiana in his honor. Known for his perseverance, quick temper, and great integrity, La Salle never wavered in his attempt to find permanent settlements for France in all parts of the valley. La Salle set out for the Mississippi River two years later with four ships and more than two hundred colonists but landed by mistake in Texas.

He and his party were unable to find the mouth of the river, and after three years of wandering through northern and central Texas, his group revolted. La Salle was killed and buried along the banks of the Brazos River, his dream of unifying northern and southern French possessions unfulfilled.

New World or committed suicide. Only a few survived and reached Louisiana.

FRANCE AND ENGLAND FIGHT

After defeating the Fox, France faced another threat to its control of the Mississippi Valley—Britain. France and Britain fought a series of wars from the 1720's to the 1760's for control of colonies not only in North America but also in Africa, India, and Asia. These wars ended in North America with the French and Indian War (1754–1763; SEE French & Indian War). In the Peace of Paris of 1763, France lost to Britain all its possessions in North America east of the Mississippi River and north of New Orleans.

French attempts to settle in the Mississippi Valley had never been successful. When Britain took control, fewer than three thousand French citizens lived in the area. It would be up to Britain to make a more permanent mark on the Mississippi Valley.

Leslie V. Tischauser

Sieur de la Salle claims the Mississippi Valley for France in 1682. The territory became known as Louisiana in honor of Louis XIV.

SEE ALSO:
CARTIER & ROBERVAL
EXPEDITIONS; FOX
WARS; FRENCH &
INDIAN WAR; FRENCH
COLONIAL POLICIES;
IROQUOIS
CONFEDERACY;
LOUISIANA PURCHASE.

FURTHER READING

• Balesi, Charles J. *The Time of the French in the Heart of North America, 1673–1818.* Chicago: Alliance Française Chicago, 1992.

• Caruso, John Anthony. *The Mississippi Valley Frontier: The Age of French Exploration and Settlement.* Indianapolis, Ind.: Bobbs-Merrill, 1966.

• Delanglez, Jean. *Life and Voyages of Louis Jolliet, 1645–1700.* Chicago: Loyola University Press, 1948.

• Eccles, W. J. *France in America.* New York: Harper & Row, 1972.

• _____. *Frontenac: The Courtier Governor.* Toronto: McClelland and Stewart, 1959.

• Muhlstein, Anka. *La Salle: Explorer of the North American Frontier.* New York: Arcade, 1994.

• White, Richard. *The Middle Ground: Indians, Empires, and Republics in the Great Lakes Region, 1650–1815.* New York: Oxford University Press, 1991.

A French fur trapper in Canada during the eighteenth century. The need of these hunters to find fresh hunting territory led to French explorations in the Mississippi Valley.

VIEWPOINTS

FRENCH-INDIAN RELATIONS

French merchants and fur traders in the Mississippi Valley generally got along very well with the region's Indians, except the Fox and Iroquois. The French were traders, not permanent settlers for the most part, and Indians welcomed them for the trade goods, tobacco, firearms, and alcohol they brought with them.

The English were not as well trusted by Indians since they were seen to be farmers whose goal was permanent settlement and conquest of Indian lands. The Fox and Iroquois fought the French because these tribes had dominated the fur trade before the Europeans arrived, and the French took away a lot of their business.

Missionaries, whether French, English, or Spanish, generally had a great deal of difficulty trying to convert Indians to Christianity. They simply preferred their traditional religions. French trappers frequently married Indian women. Their children were called *brules* or metis.

Missouri Compromise

Henry Clay addresses the U.S. Senate in 1850. He negotiated both the Missouri Compromise in 1820 and the Great Compromise of 1850, which held the Union together after a split threatened over the issue of slavery.

The Missouri Compromise, approved by Congress on March 3, 1820, ended the first great crisis over slavery in the nineteenth century. This conflict began on February 13, 1819, when a New York congressman, James Tallmadge, introduced a bill that would have limited slavery in the state. The bill barred slaves from entering Missouri after the state was admitted to the Union and freed all slaves born after admission when they reached the age of twenty-five. Tallmadge's proposal sparked a yearlong debate between the North and the South over Missouri and the expansion of slavery.

In 1819, the bill passed the Northern-dominated House of Representatives but failed in the Senate, where Southerners and their Northern allies defeated it. This voting demonstrated the sectional split between North and South that, forty years later, helped to cause the Civil War. When Congress returned in 1820, the conflict between the two sections over the admission of Missouri continued.

A compromise, negotiated by Speaker of the House Henry Clay, was reached between Northern and Southern congressmen when it was agreed to admit the state of Maine, then part of Massachusetts, without slavery and to admit Missouri as a slave state. The admission of Missouri and Maine gave both the North and the South an equal number of states in the Union and an equal number of senators in the United States Congress. This balance in the Senate was desirable, as it gave the South the power to block any legislation detrimental to its interests.

Furthermore, slavery was outlawed in the remainder of the Louisiana Territory north of 36° 30', the southern border of Missouri. The vast area north of this line, which ran westward into the Great Plains, was opened for the creation of free states, and the area south of this line, including Arkansas, Oklahoma, and Texas, would be organized as slave states. Missouri was admitted to the Union in 1821.

Jeff R. Bremer

CAUSES AND EFFECTS

After the Louisiana Purchase, thousands of settlers flooded westward into areas such as Missouri. Southerners who brought their slaves with them wanted Missouri admitted as a slave state, and Northerners wished to halt the territorial expansion of slavery.

The Missouri Compromise served as a sectional truce between North and South. The expansion of slavery was limited to south of the 36° 30' line, but the political conflict did not end. The annexation of Texas, California, and other Western territories in the 1840's once again brought up the question of whether slavery would be allowed in new territories.

SEE ALSO:
CIVIL WAR; LOUISIANA PURCHASE; SLAVERY IN THE AMERICAS; WESTWARD EXPANSION.

Monroe Doctrine

James Monroe, as U.S. president, espoused the Monroe Doctrine, which blocked further European colonization in the Americas.

SUMMARY

➤ In the early 1820's, Americans feared European intervention in the New World.
➤ President James Monroe set forth the Monroe Doctrine in 1823.
➤ The doctrine contained four key concepts: exceptionalism, noncolonization, noninterference, and neutrality.
➤ The doctrine was used in the twentieth century to justify American intervention in Central and South America and the Caribbean.

Arguably the most significant foreign policy pronouncement in United States history, the Monroe Doctrine began in an interplay of weakness, bravado, defensiveness, expansionism, and opportunism. Since independence, Americans had worried about the continued and possibly hostile presence of Britain, France, Spain, and Russia in the New World. However, rapprochement with Britain followed the War of 1812, and France had already departed North America by selling Louisiana in 1803. Only the Spanish Floridas, West Indies, New Spain (Mexico), and Russian possessions in the Pacific Northwest remained as possible threats or impediments. For decades, the United States had sought to acquire Florida and Cuba,

which together lay across the main trade route between New Orleans and the Atlantic. Secretary of State John Quincy Adams won American possession of the Floridas after difficult negotiations from 1818 to 1821. Negotiations dragged on as Spain insisted that the United States deny diplomatic recognition to Latin American colonial rebels. Adams agreed, but by 1822, the United States, wishing to trade with its neighbors, recognized the newly independent Latin American states. No European government followed its lead. Some Americans wondered if there were European plans to reconquer Spain's lost empire.

NEW WORLD INTERVENTION FEARED

Russian czar Alexander I embodied the United States' fears. In 1814, he had founded a continental Holy Alliance, and he intended to suppress revolutionary liberalism and restore monarchism throughout Europe. The czar also envisaged Russian Alaska as running south down the Pacific Coast, overlapping territories claimed by the United States or Britain.

Recovering Spain's former colonies would suit the mood and ideals of conservative European monarchies, which since 1815 had also backed a restored kingdom in France. In April 1823 France sent armies into Spain to put down a revolution.

Britain, seeing vast commercial opportunities in the former Spanish empire, confronted the Holy Alliance and actively opposed reconquest. Soon after French troops invaded Spain, Britain warned France to withdraw and advised against planning intervention in the New World.

Britain wanted permanent Latin American independence although it withheld recognition of the new Latin American states. British foreign secretary George Canning met in August 1823 with

American ambassador Richard Rush to ask him if his government would consider a joint Anglo-American policy.

Canning's offer contained a fatal flaw. Britain insisted on what it called a "no-transfer" principle, designed to prevent any of Spain's former possessions from being turned over to another empire. Rush and the U.S. government could not accept this because it would have prevented future annexation of Texas and Cuba. Rush nonetheless sent Canning's offer to Washington.

Meanwhile Canning continued negotiations with France. In October 1823 he received from France the Polignac Pledge, whereby that country renounced any designs in America. Unaware of France's pledge, President James Monroe, Secretary of State Adams, and other policymakers began in November to weigh Canning's offer.

Adams strongly opposed aligning with Britain, viewing it as confining and embarrassing. He favored a unilateral statement, applying to both the Holy Alliance powers and Britain, whose failure to recognize the newly independent Latin American republics could be seen as ominous. Monroe's other major advisers from former presidents Thomas Jefferson and James Madison to Secretary of War John C. Calhoun counseled accepting the joint proposal. President Monroe ultimately sided with Adams.

THE DOCTRINE ANNOUNCED

On December 2, 1823, Monroe enunciated what would be known as the Monroe Doctrine. It contained four key concepts: exceptionalism, noncolonization, noninterference, and neutrality. Monroe declared that the Americas and Europe ought to remain separate because European monarchism in this hemisphere would pose a danger to the United States. Henceforth (after 330 years of conquest and settlement), the Western Hemisphere would be closed to establishment of new European colonies. In return, the United States would not interfere with existing European possessions in the hemisphere and would remain uninvolved in European wars and rivalries. Monroe's new policy, not yet a doctrine, was denounced by some European statesmen and ignored by others. Americans quickly forgot Monroe's "doctrine," and Monroe himself did not consider it an enduring maxim.

In the nineteenth century, the doctrine was rarely invoked, even though European states often intervened in Latin America.

The fear that rivals such as Czar Alexander I would engage in territorial expansion on the American continent encouraged the United States to draft the Monroe Doctrine. It was designed to prevent colonial powers encroaching on the territory of the United States or its neighbors.

VIEWPOINTS

MONROE DOCTRINE JUSTIFIES INTERVENTION

In 1848 Spain and Britain contemplated establishing a protectorate in the Yucatán Peninsula. President James K. Polk, having just defeated Mexico, announced that the United States would assume control itself to prevent European encroachment.

This act, which foreshadowed the Olney (1895) and Roosevelt (1904) Corollaries, marked the first Monroe Doctrine sanctioning of U.S. intervention in Latin America. In the 1980's, the doctrine was invoked again to justify President Ronald Reagan's intervention in Nicaragua.

SEE ALSO:
ADAMS-ONÍS TREATY;
CUBAN REPUBLIC;
CUBAN REVOLUTION;
DOLLAR DIPLOMACY;
THE FRENCH IN
MEXICO; GOOD
NEIGHBOR POLICY;
HOOVER'S PRESIDENCY;
MEXICAN-AMERICAN
WAR; NICARAGUAN
CIVIL WAR;
NICARAGUAN
INTERVENTION;
ORGANIZATION OF
AMERICAN STATES;
SALVADORAN CIVIL
WAR.

President James K. Polk cited it during the Mexican-American War (SEE Mexican-American War) and again in a dispute with Britain over constructing an isthmian canal. In the 1860's Secretary of State William Seward used it when Spain intervened in Santo Domingo and when France set up a puppet state in Mexico under the Emperor Maximilian (SEE The French in Mexico).

THE DOCTRINE IN THE TWENTIETH CENTURY

Burgeoning U.S. power and pride near the turn of the century resulted in fundamental redefinitions. The Olney (1895) and Roosevelt (1904) Corollaries, resulting from the First and Second Venezuelan Crises, would be used repeatedly until the 1930's to justify U.S. armed intervention in South American, Central American, and Caribbean nations and full or partial protectorates of Cuba (1898–1934), Nicaragua (1909–1933), Haiti (1915–1941), and the Dominican Republic (1905–1941) (SEE Cuban Republic; Nicaraguan Intervention). Inter- vention had become very important in U.S. foreign policy.

From the 1930's until the 1980's, the United States retreated somewhat from its role as police of the hemisphere. Presidents Herbert Hoover and Franklin Delano Roosevelt wooed Latin Americans with a Good Neighbor Policy (1933) that renounced rights to intervene in another nation's affairs (SEE Good Neighbor Policy).

From World War II until the 1980's, the United States trod lightly (or covertly) in Latin America, even after Fidel Castro turned Cuba communist (SEE Cuban Revolution). In the Cold War, the United States remained cautious, intervening under sanction of the Organization of American States (SEE Organization of American States). In the 1980's, however, Presidents Ronald Reagan and George Bush partially reversed this trend. In response to "indirect Soviet aggression" in El Salvador and Nicaragua, for example, Reagan intervened to sustain pro-U.S. forces (SEE Nicaraguan Civil War; Salvadoran Civil War).

Ken Millen-Penn

FURTHER READING

•Combs, Jerald A. "The Diplomacy of Expansion." In *The History of American Foreign Policy*. New York: McGraw-Hill, 1997.

•May, Ernest R. *The Making of the Monroe Doctrine*. Cambridge, Mass.: Harvard University Press, 1975.

•Perkins, Dexter. *A History of the Monroe Doctrine*. Boston: Little, Brown, 1963.

European leaders gaze on U.S. naval might assembled under the Monroe Doctrine in a New York Herald *cartoon.*

Montgomery Bus Boycott

Rosa Parks, an African-American, arrives at court in Montgomery, Alabama, in March 1956, ready to face charges of violating the law by refusing to relinquish her seat to a white American.

Segregation of the races in public facilities throughout the Southern United States was the norm during the Jim Crow era (1880's–1950's; SEE Jim Crow Laws). The Civil Rights movement, however, began to change that. Among the earliest civil-rights battles was the Montgomery Bus Boycott.

On December 1, 1955, Rosa Parks, an African-American seamstress and former secretary of the local branch of the National Association for the Advancement of Colored People (NAACP), was arrested in the city of Montgomery, Alabama, for refusing to relinquish her seat on a municipal bus.

Local ordinance required that African-American passengers pay their fare in the front of the bus, then board the bus at the rear. African-Americans were required to sit in the back of the bus and to remain standing if all seats in the section for blacks were full even if seats in the section for whites were empty. In addition, African-Americans were required to give up their seats at the front

boundary of the black section when the bus was full and additional white passengers boarded. This was the situation in which Parks found herself.

THE BOYCOTT

The news of Parks' arrest spread quickly, and by that evening E. D. Nixon, local head of the NAACP, and Jo Ann Robinson, an English instructor at Alabama State College and head of the Women's Political Council, had devised plans to boycott the city's buses. The Women's Political Council was chiefly responsible for distributing forty thousand handbills announcing the boycott. Nixon contacted the young and unknown Reverend Martin Luther King, Jr., who, along with the Reverend Ralph Abernathy and other African-American ministers, had offered his help (SEE King's Assassination). On Sunday, December 4, African-American ministers all over Montgomery urged their parishioners not to ride the bus the next day and to attend

SUMMARY

➤ In December 1955, African-American Rosa Parks refused to give up a seat on a segregated Montgomery, Alabama, bus and was arrested.
➤ The NAACP organized a bus boycott and asked the Reverend Martin Luther King, Jr., to head the protest.
➤ In January, the group demanded complete desegregation of buses.
➤ In November 1956 the Supreme Court affirmed a lower court's ruling, invalidating local laws regarding segregated seating on buses.
➤ On December 21, 1956, the buses throughout Montgomery were desegregated.

Eight of the eighty-nine African-American bus boycott leaders who were arrested in Montgomery on February 22, 1956.

CAUSES AND EFFECTS

Despite the elimination of slavery ninety years earlier, African-Americans faced a great deal of oppression, discrimination, and ill treatment in the Southern United States in the 1950's, including the widespread insistence by the white community on segregating the races in all spheres of public life. Segregation in municipal buses was one of many examples of segregated accommodations. The Montgomery Bus Boycott is widely seen as one of the two catalyzing events of the Civil Rights movement, the other being the Supreme Court's decision in *Brown v. Board of Education.* Because a yearlong nonviolent bus boycott was successful in eliminating all segregation in municipal public transit, this battle gave strength and moral courage to civil-rights activists to attempt to desegregate other avenues of American life. Another important effect of the Montgomery Bus Boycott was that it brought Martin Luther King, Jr., into the public eye and into the leadership of the Civil Rights movement.

a mass meeting Monday evening for further instructions. The active mobilization by the churches brought an important new element into the fight for civil rights: mass mobilization that was deeply rooted in spirituality.

The Monday bus boycott was so successful that African-American citizens decided to form an organization whose purpose would be to run a boycott of the buses for as long as it took to achieve three goals. The organization was named the Montgomery Improvement Association (MIA), and King was asked to head it. At the mass meeting Monday night, King enunciated the three demands of the MIA and the ongoing boycott: courteous treatment by bus drivers toward African-American passengers; first-come, first-served seating on buses, with whites filling the front and African-Americans the rear of the bus; and some employment of African-American bus drivers on predominantly African-American routes.

The bus boycott dragged on for weeks while city leaders refused to negotiate any changes in the policies. African-American leaders were arrested, and on January 30, 1956, King's house was dynamited. These actions only solidified the determination of the civil-rights activists, and they decided to press for greater changes than those they had initially demanded. They wanted complete desegregation of the buses.

As the boycott wore on, African-Americans in the city learned how to walk or carpool wherever they wanted to go. The bus company, whose ridership had been 75 percent African-American, saw a serious downturn in profits, as did many merchants who now saw fewer African-American shoppers because of the difficulty of getting to the stores.

Inspiring and motivating speeches by King and rousing gospel songs filled with images of freedom and determination sustained the protesters at mass meetings held in churches several times a week.

THE COURTS RULE

Five months into the boycott, on May 11, 1956, the United States District Court heard the suit contesting public transportation segregation laws and declared the city's bus ordinance unconstitutional. The City of Montgomery appealed, and the boycott continued. On November 13, 1956, the United States Supreme Court affirmed the ruling of the District Court, thus invalidating local laws regarding segregated seating on buses. It took more than a month for the federal court order to reach Montgomery, but on December 21, 1956—one day after the court order arrived— the buses throughout Montgomery were desegregated.

Lisa Langenbach

TURNING POINT

FREEDOM RIDERS (1961)

Although the United States Supreme Court had in 1946 declared segregated seating in interstate transportation unconstitutional and in 1960 declared segregated waiting rooms in interstate bus terminals unconstitutional, in 1961 segregation in interstate transportation was still widely practiced throughout the South. The Freedom Rides were a series of attempts to eliminate segregation in interstate transportation.

Beginning on May 4, 1961, an interracial group of thirteen riders boarded a bus in Washington, D.C., for a trip through most of the Southern states, ending in New Orleans, Louisiana. Before starting their journey, the Freedom Riders had notified the United States Justice Department, President John F. Kennedy, and the heads of Greyhound and Trailways bus lines that they were planning to practice nonviolent civil disobedience deliberately violating Southern segregation laws regarding seating both on the bus and in waiting areas at each bus terminal. They received no reply from any of those whom they had notified, and so proceeded with their ride. Alerted that they were on their way, cities in Virginia and North Carolina quickly complied with the law and removed signs designating "white only" and "colored" waiting areas in their bus terminals.

Over the course of several months, more than a thousand individuals took part in Freedom Rides. However, resistance to federal law was strong in the Deep South. Much violence was directed at the Freedom Riders and the buses on which they rode. In Alabama, one bus was firebombed, and riders were beaten and bloodied in South Carolina, Alabama, and Mississippi. Despite the violence directed at them, protesters remained committed to nonviolence. With the help of President Kennedy and federal marshals sent to keep the peace and a decree from the Interstate Commerce Commission banning segregation in interstate transportation, the Freedom Riders succeeded in their mission.

SEE ALSO:
BROWN V. BOARD OF EDUCATION; CIVIL RIGHTS MOVEMENT; EMANCIPATION PROCLAMATION; JIM CROW LAWS; KENNEDY'S PRESIDENCY; KING'S ASSASSINATION.

FURTHER READING

•Garrow, David J., ed. *The Walking City: The Montgomery Bus Boycott, 1955–1956.* Brooklyn, N.Y.: Carlson, 1989.

•King, Martin Luther, Jr. *Stride Toward Freedom: The Montgomery Story.* New York: Harper and Bros., 1958.

•Raines, Howell. *My Soul Is Rested: The Story of the Civil Rights Movement in the Deep South, Told by the Men and Women Who Made it Happen.* New York: G. P. Putnam's Sons, 1977.

•Robinson, Jo Ann Gibson. *The Montgomery Bus Boycott and the Women Who Started It: The Memoir of Jo Ann Gibson Robinson.* Edited by David J. Garrow. Knoxville: University of Tennessee Press, 1987.

The Reverend Martin Luther King, Jr., (right), leader of the Montgomery Bus Boycott, celebrates victory in the dispute by riding a Montgomery bus up front along with the Reverend Glenn Smiley of Texas.

Mormon Settlement of Utah

A Mormon pioneer family is photographed outside their home in Echo City, Utah, in 1869, two decades after the state was first settled by members of the religion.

SUMMARY

➤ The members of the Church of Jesus Christ of Latter-day Saints (Mormon Church) left Nauvoo, Illinois, in February 1846 to avoid persecution.
➤ They set up temporary encampments in Iowa and Nebraska.
➤ The first group of Mormons, a company of 148 led by Brigham Young, arrived in the Salt Lake Valley in 1847.
➤ Five companies followed, and the Mormons in the Great Basin set up a community and prepared for the others, who arrived in 1848.

Members of the Church of Jesus Christ of Latter-day Saints (Mormon Church) had planned to leave Nauvoo, Illinois, in spring 1846, and travel toward the Rocky Mountains to establish a new home and avoid persecution. However, the hostile environment forced a small group of church leaders and members to leave Nauvoo on February 4. Despite the frigid conditions, more than 2,000 Mormons fled Nauvoo within a few weeks. By September, approximately 16,000 were in Iowa, waiting to follow Brigham Young, Joseph Smith's successor, to the Rocky Mountains. This massive Mormon migration occurred during a period of continental expansion in the United States, and Mormons played a crucial role in settlement of the West.

In 1842, Smith prophesied that his followers would settle in the Rocky Mountains. Mormons hoped to settle in an area where they could practice their religious beliefs without interference.

After leaving Nauvoo, Mormons organized a small encampment across the Mississippi River at Sugar Creek, Iowa. They organized other encampments in Iowa Garden Grove, Mount Pisgah, and Council Bluffs and at Winter Quarters in Nebraska.

Young desperately wanted a small expedition to reach the Great Basin in 1846, but external forces frustrated his plan. The winter of 1846–1847 was extremely cold. Temperatures dipped below zero, hindering movement and claiming many casualties. Furthermore, most families lacked adequate supplies and equipment for the journey. Exacerbating Young's difficulties, five hundred able-bodied men joined the U.S. Army in July 1846 to fight in the Mexican-American War (SEE Mexican-American War). Consequently, Mormons did not reach the Great Basin until 1847.

By spring 1847, Young organized a vanguard company of 148 men, women, and children, including 3 African-Americans. On the trail, Young contracted mountain fever. He remained behind but sent a smaller advance company ahead to enter the Salt Lake Valley. This advance company of 42 men pushed its way into the valley via the Donner-Reed Trail. Two scouts entered the Salt Lake Valley on July 21. The remaining members arrived the next day. These men located the best land for farming and began irrigating, plowing, and planting crops by July 23. Young's party reached the Salt Lake Valley on July 24. Young reportedly looked out of his wagon toward the valley and told his carriage driver: "This is the right place, drive on." Young and a few others later returned to the Mormon encampments in Nebraska and Iowa. They spent the winter months organizing companies to travel to the Salt Lake Valley the next summer.

Five other companies of Mormon pioneers journeyed west in 1847. Members of these companies, recently discharged Mormon Battalion soldiers, and those who arrived in the first company prepared for the next year's arrivals. Nearly two thousand people spent the winter of 1847–1848 in the Salt Lake Valley, planting crops, constructing an irrigation system, building homes, and exploring the surrounding territory. The settlers divided into work committees that irrigated, plowed, and sowed crops; planned and surveyed the city; found and retrieved timber for building; constructed roads; erected buildings; and built corrals. They also established sawmills and flour mills and opened blacksmith and tannery shops.

Mormons regarded natural resources, such as water, timber, and land, as objects of stewardship. Clergy leaders regulated these publicly owned commodities for the benefit of all. Furthermore, Young insisted that none of his followers engage in land speculation; families who arrived in the territory received land based on their circumstances and needs at no charge.

These early settlers enjoyed a relatively mild winter, allowing them to continue plowing and planting. However, late-spring frosts destroyed many vegetable and grain crops. Hordes of crickets descended on the remaining crops. Shortly after the crickets arrived, gulls flew into the fields and gorged themselves on the insects, saving some of the crops. Settlers, however, had to resort to consuming edible flowers and roots to avoid starvation. Only portions of the devastated

CAUSES AND EFFECTS

After lawless mobs murdered Joseph Smith, Mormonism's founder and leader, in Nauvoo, Illinois, on June 27, 1844, tensions subsided briefly but then returned and escalated. Mobs harassed Mormons, destroying crops, stealing belongings, and assaulting individuals. Members of the Church of Jesus Christ of Latter-day Saints agreed to move for the fourth time in sixteen years in spring 1846. However, mob threats persisted, and false accusations against Mormon Church leaders necessitated an earlier exodus. Mormons left Illinois and organized several camps in Iowa and Nebraska. They traveled north of the Platte River, on the Mormon Trail, and migrated to their new home in the Salt Lake Valley.

crops survived the summer drought, and a small harvest was produced in July.

In May 1848, Young organized nearly two thousand followers into three companies to migrate from eastern Nebraska to the Rocky Mountains. They brought mules, oxen, cows, sheep, goats, pigs, chickens, geese, beehives, cats, and dogs to the Great Basin.

The first two companies arrived in September; the last reached the Salt Lake Valley in mid-October. Members of these companies effectively doubled the valley's

Brigham Young led Mormons to Utah after religious persecution in Missouri and Illinois had forced them to seek a new, safer home.

FURTHER READING

•Allen, James B., and Glen M. Leonard. *The Story of the Latter-day Saints.* Salt Lake City: Deseret Book Company, 1976.

•Arrington, Leonard J. *Brigham Young: American Moses.* New York: Alfred A. Knopf, 1985.

•Arrington, Leonard J., and Davis Bitton. *The Mormon Experience.* 2d ed. Urbana: University of Illinois Press, 1992.

•Hunter, Milton R. *Utah: The Story of Her People.* Salt Lake City: Deseret News Press, 1946.

•Poll, Richard D., Thomas G. Alexander, Eugene E. Campbell, and David E. Miller, eds. *Utah's History.* Logan: Utah State University Press, 1989.

•Stegner, Wallace. *The Gathering of Zion: The Story of the Mormon Trail.* New York: McGraw-Hill, 1964.

DAILY LIFE

LIFE ON THE MORMON TRAIL

Young instructed his followers to organize into companies of tens, fifties, and hundreds before traveling west. Company officers managed each level and reported to a presiding authority and his two counselors.

All companies maintained strict schedules, rising before dawn, holding morning and evening prayers, marching all day, making camp at night, and keeping the Sabbath holy. Constant walking took its toll on the infirm, the young, and the elderly.

Sickness and death punctuated life along the trail. Between August 1846 and July 1848 several hundred people on the Mormon Trail died from exposure, scurvy, malaria, and consumption. Eliza R. Snow described conditions along the trail: "Nursing the sick in tents and wagons was a laborious service, but the patient faithfulness with which it was performed is, no doubt, registered in the archives above. . . . The burial of the dead by the wayside was a sad office. For husbands, wives and children to consign the cherished remains of loved ones to a lone, desert grave, was enough to try the firmest heart-strings."

One of Snow's contemporaries, John D. Halladay, noted that some people gradually became desensitized to death: "The burials from our company had become so frequent, that they lost much of their saddening power; or, rather, we refused to retain so deeply the sadness, throwing it off in self-defense."

Mormons leaving Nauvoo, Illinois, to make their way west in 1846.

population. Some began spreading out beyond the original settlement. Because virtually all area settlers were affiliated with the Mormon Church, the first government was intermeshed with the Mormon ecclesiastical system. Settlers lived under a theocracy from 1847 to 1849. Church leaders functioned as both religious and political authorities, performing their duties free of charge.

Mormons transplanted their culture and community to their new home in the Utah territory. They helped settle vast portions of western America and improved irrigation and farming techniques in the arid Southwestern desert (SEE Westward Expansion). Mormons created a thriving society in spite of formidable obstacles.

Heather M. Seferovich

Mulroney's Ministry

Canadian prime minister Brian Mulroney (right) with U.S. president Ronald Reagan. Mulroney was keen to improve relations between Canada and the United States.

SUMMARY

➤ Brian Mulroney, a relative outsider to politics, was elected on September 4, 1984, as Conservative prime minister of Canada.
➤ The Canadian people sought national economic improvement and a change from Liberal policies.
➤ Mulroney took measures to improve the Canadian economy, increase Canada's military strength, and improve relations with the United States.
➤ Although enjoying some success in all these areas, Mulroney's ministry did not succeed in solving the constitutional issues involving Quebec, and unemployment continued to trouble the electorate.
➤ In the face of waning support for the Conservatives, Mulroney called for an election in 1988, a year sooner than required, and won.
➤ Mulroney, faced with difficulties in maintaining Canada's national spending, instituted an unpopular new Goods and Services Tax in 1991.
➤ Mulroney continued his economic and foreign policies, giving support to the North American Free Trade Agreement with the United States and Mexico in 1993.
➤ The NAFTA agreement displeased many Canadians, and Mulroney, facing polls indicating his increasing unpopularity, stepped down in 1993, to be succeed by Kim Campbell.

Brian Mulroney's Conservative Party government in Canada held power for a decade, from September 4, 1984, to February 24, 1993. Mulroney enjoyed two record-setting election victories. Mulroney's lengthy tenure in office began with high popularity but witnessed declining effectiveness and public support by the early 1990's.

Born March 20, 1939, in Quebec, Mulroney did not suggest, in his early life, a strong political orientation. After university education, he earned a law degree and began a legal career in 1962. He eventually entered the business and corporate world, and by 1977 became president of a mining company. His interests eventually gravitated toward politics, and Mulroney became an active member of the Conservative Party.

Although lacking political experience, he had sought the leadership of the party in 1976 and was defeated by Joe Clark, an established and respected party colleague. Mulroney's failure, however, indicated his strong personality and a determination to succeed. Several years later the Conservatives, struggling under eighteen years of Liberal Party rule, gravitated to Mulroney in his second effort. In June, 1983, seeing Mulroney as a fresh personality who might give better results, the Conservative Party selected him to lead.

Between 1980 and 1984, still out of power and serving as the primary opposition to the Liberal ministry, the Conservatives prepared for the next national election. The opportunity looked favorable, due to a period of budget deficits, economic recession, and turmoil within the Liberal Party. In September 1984, the Conservative Party won an impressive 211 of 282 seats in the lower house, the largest majority to that time in Canadian political history. The Conservatives were also victorious in every province. In accordance with parliamentary practice, Mulroney, as party head, became

Brian Mulroney inserts his ballot for the 1988 parliamentary election. Despite concerns over falling popularity ratings he was reelected as prime minister of Canada.

prime minister of Canada, and he took the oath of office on September 17, 1984.

THE NEW ADMINISTRATION

The forty-five-year-old Mulroney selected his cabinet and embarked on his domestic and foreign policy agenda. His ministry of thirty-nine members, including six women, was the largest in the nation's history. Canada's sluggish economy demanded immediate attention, as problems inherited from the former ministry included the debilitating effects of a recession during the early 1980's. Significant unemployment and government deficits challenged the new ministry. A central issue was the federal obligation to

support the impressive system of social services for which Canada had become internationally famous. Federal programs included a national health care system guaranteed to all Canadian citizens, educational opportunities, job training, pensions, and support for the Indian population.

In foreign policy, the Liberals had reduced Canada's financial support of and commitment of personnel to the North Atlantic Treaty Organization (SEE North Atlantic Treaty). The Conservatives were concerned at the message that such reduction conveyed to the Soviet Union and its allies. In addition, relations with the United States of America had been uneven. Brian Mulroney and the Conservatives were determined to create a stronger Canadian military and develop closer, more substantial ties to NATO. The government announced ambitious plans for substantial increases in the military budget, significant expansion of military forces, purchase of weapons, and greater strength and visibility as part of NATO forces. In foreign policy, a strong anti-Soviet stance quickly emerged as a policy parallel to the promised increases in Canada's military posture.

Improving the economy, however, proved more difficult than had been anticipated. The planned expansion of the Canadian military, outlined in a detailed report, eventually had to be substantially reduced. The main thrust of the Mulroney agenda continued, nevertheless, and several economic indicators in his first term showed positive results compared to the pre-1984 era. Unemployment between 1984 and 1988, for example, gradually decreased nationally. One noteworthy aspect of Mulroney's lengthy tenure in office involved Canada's relations with the United States during the administrations of Ronald Reagan and George Bush. The Canadian prime minister and the two American leaders met periodically, beginning in March 1985, and genuine friendship encouraged bilateral cooperation on many issues. A major goal of both nations was trade expansion, and during the Mulroney years a number of steps assisted this common objective. The two governments signed a free-trade agreement (FTA) in 1987, which became effective in early 1989. Negotiations in 1991–1992 to expand the FTA to include Mexico evolved into the North American Free Trade Agreement, ratified in 1993 (SEE NAFTA).

These closer ties and economic integration with the United States led to concerns within the Canadian public and business communities. The Canadian dollar continued its weak position against the U.S. dollar in 1985 and 1986, and free trade became a political issue. The Liberals criticized the Canadian-U.S. free-trade agreements as leading to a loss of Canadian jobs, a weakening of the economy, and the decline of Canadian sovereignty. The Liberals' protectionist arguments found receptive listeners and put Mulroney on the defensive. Public opinion polls in 1986 showed a decline in Canadian support of free trade with the United States. The political fortunes of the Conservatives felt the brunt of growing discontent in other ways. At the provincial level the Conservatives lost power in Prince Edward Island in 1986. The same year, although the party retained power in Alberta, it lost seats in the provincial legisla-

ture. Mulroney's own popularity in the national polls dropped in the summer of 1986, as the majority of respondents expressed a wish for a new prime minister and a different party in power. In 1987, political foes intensified their criticism of the Conservative record. Western dissatisfaction with Ottawa and the Mulroney policies grew significantly. One manifestation of this mood was the creation of the Reform Party, located primarily in Alberta but seeking to tap a broader base of public support opposed to the Conservative Party.

SECOND TERM

Mulroney took a calculated gamble to confront his opposition by calling a parliamentary election in 1988, a year earlier than required. His decision proved to be correct. The free trade issue quickly became the centerpiece of the campaign of both major

Brian Mulroney with (from left to rigtht) British prime minister Margaret Thatcher, U.S. president Ronald Reagan, and French president Francois Mitterand at the 1988 G-7 Economic Summit.

TEMPER OF THE TIMES

EXPO '86

Vancouver, British Columbia, served as the host city for the world's fair known as Expo '86, lasting from May to October 1986. The event celebrated the centennial of the western Canadian city. The massive undertaking took several years to plan, prepare, and build the necessary facilities, all at a cost of roughly $1.6 billion in U.S. dollars. Critics pointed to a study that the fair would lose hundreds of millions of dollars and that the debt from Montreal Expo of 1967 was still being paid.

Less tangible but equally significant gains were to be made, however: Canadian and British Columbian pride was enhanced, and disparate groups came together to complete the project, which businessman James Pattison and provincial premier William Bennet ran well. More than twenty-two million visitors enjoyed the exhibits and programs and gave a major boost to the important trade center, which opens to the Pacific Ocean and Asia.

The Expo Center and Monorail at the World Expo '86, held in Vancouver.

parties. The majority of the electorate, however, stayed with Mulroney and his administration, returning the Conservatives to power in November 1988. Although Mulroney's party lost seats in the House of Commons, it still held an absolute majority. The Conservatives had won their first "back-to-back" election victory in a century. This new electoral mandate would seem to have been good news for the Conservatives.

Unfortunately for Brian Mulroney, however, his second term revealed many social and economic difficulties that his government could not easily solve.

Economic indicators continued to fall or remain stagnant, and by 1993, Canadians were aware that they were experiencing the longest recession of the post-World War II era. Unemployment remained steady at over 11 percent, accompanied by record numbers of personal and business bankruptcies.

Public demonstrations and even minor outbreaks of violence showed the strains facing many Canadians. Continued budget deficits raised growing concerns about the administration's ability to govern effectively. The Canadian dollar remained weak, especially as compared to the American dollar, and this affected trade and investments. Unpopular revenue measures, notably the new 1991 goods and services tax, eroded public support and confidence.

Disagreements over the positive and negative effects of the NAFTA arose again during the period of economic sluggishness. Mulroney's opponents took this opportunity to portray him as being tied too closely to the Americans and consequently not defending Canada's economic and national interests vigorously enough.

The political opposition gained strength during Mulroney's second term, illustrated by the New Democratic Party's victory in the 1990 provincial election in Ontario over the Liberals and Conservatives (SEE Canadian Political Parties). A socialist administration now governed Canada's largest province.

As if economic issues were not challenging enough, the subject of federal-provincial relations revealed even more fundamental problems. Brian Mulroney's regime sought to address these concerns, especially those of Quebec, and negotiated the Meech Lake agreement in 1987. Lack of sufficient support from all provinces negated the accord in 1990. A second effort, outlined in the Charlottetown Accord, failed to convince the majority of Canadian voters in a 1992 national referendum.

Consequently, the problems and disputes related to the status of Quebec and other provinces were not resolved during Brian

VIEWPOINTS

SHOULD QUEBEC LEAVE CANADA?

The history of Quebec province within Canada is a long and complicated one. Quebec's French heritage and culture occasionally led to frictions and misunderstandings with other provinces and the national government. Wishing to be treated as a distinct society, Quebec sought federal rights to protect its sovereignty and distinct culture. Many in Quebec even preferred independence from Canada. Other provinces, however, objected to granting, in the Canadian constitution, rights to Quebec that other provinces did not enjoy. This led to political stalemate and constitutional crisis. The failures of the government's proposed reforms in 1990 and 1992 to meet Quebec's concerns meant that the problems and disputes related to Quebec's status were passed to Mulroney's successors.

Mulroney's tenure as prime minister (SEE Quebec Sovereignist Movement).

The next parliamentary election had to occur no later than 1993, and public opinion polls by early 1993 showed growing opposition to the Conservatives. Especially low support in the polls for Mulroney as prime minister added to the party's woes, suggesting that his continuation would be a definite liability. Consequently, in February 1993, he announced his intention to resign after a successor had been selected. Kim Campbell, a member of his cabinet, replaced Mulroney as prime minister in June (SEE Campbell's Ministry). At age fifty-three, he could move on to other interests.

THE MINISTRY IN REVIEW

Mulroney made many contributions to his country, but the record of this energetic and capable national leader is mixed. Efforts, only partially successful, to control ballooning government programs and expenditures in a period of fiscal limitations were paralleled in other leading industrial nations in Europe and North America.

Good relations with the U.S., in trade and overall foreign policy, continued the historical pattern of friendship and cooperation between the two nations, but disputes and disagreements did not totally disappear. Under his leadership, Canada continued its active involvement in foreign affairs and international trade, but fell short of reaching its objective as a dominant world leader.

Taylor Stults

Old Quebec in the capital of Quebec province, where the debate over sovereignty has long been a major issue in Canadian politics.

SEE ALSO:
CAMPBELL'S MINISTRY; CANADIAN POLITICAL PARTIES; NAFTA; NORTH ATLANTIC TREATY; QUEBEC SOVEREIGNIST MOVEMENT; U.S.-CANADIAN RELATIONS.

FURTHER READING

•Frizzell, Alan, and Anthony Westell. *The Canadian General Election of 1984.* Ottawa: Carleton University Press, 1985.

•MacDonald, L. Ian. *Mulroney: The Making of the Prime Minister.* Toronto: McClelland and Stewart, 1984.

•Martin, Lawrence. *Pledge of Allegiance: The Americanization of Canada in the Mulroney Years.* Toronto: McClelland and Stewart, 1993.

•Sawatsky, John. *Mulroney: The Politics of Ambition.* Toronto: Macfarlane Walter and Ross, 1991.

•Tomlin, Brian W., and Maureen A. Molot, eds. *Canada Among Nations: The Tory Record, 1988.* Toronto: James Lorimer, 1989.

Multiculturalism Act of Canada

Chinatown in Vancouver reflects the rich diversity of Canadian society.

The 1988 Multiculturalism Act of Canada recognizes and promotes the understanding of multiculturalism in a diverse Canadian society and allows its citizens the right to preserve, enhance, and share their cultural heritage. The act confirms that multiculturalism is a fundamental characteristic of Canada's heritage, promotes full and equitable participation of individuals and communities of all origins in the continuing evolution and shaping of all aspects of Canadian society, recognizes and enhances the development of communities that share a common origin, and ensures that cultural diversity is respected under the law and by Canada's social, cultural, economic, and political institutions. It generates understanding and creativity through the interaction of individuals and communities, fosters the recognition and appreciation of diverse cultures, and preserves and enhances the use of languages other than English and French.

The act obligates the federal institutions of Canada to ensure that all Canadians have equal employment and advancement opportunities; promotes policies, programs, and practices that enhance the ability of individuals and communities of all origins to maintain diversity within Canada's evolution; collects data on programs and practices that are sensitive and responsive to Canada's multiculturalism; and utilizes language skills and cultural understanding to benefit each Canadian citizen regardless of origin. Canadian Government policy encourages and assists individuals, organizations, and institutions that want to conduct research, promote exchanges, and encourage the preservation, sharing, and knowledge of Canadian diversity.

The minister for multiculturalism facilitates the acquisition, retention, and use of all languages that reflect Canada's multicultural heritage; works to end discrimination based on race or national or ethnic origin; and implements all federal policies designed to promote multiculturalism in Canada. The minister may enter agreements with provincial governments, foreign governments, and establish advisory committees with intent to foster and implement multiculturalism. Multicultural expenditures, appropriated by Parliament, are annually reviewed along with multicultural policy.

William A. Paquette

CAUSES AND EFFECTS

The Multiculturalism Act of Canada was designed to ensure that no Canadian is denied the opportunity to fully participate in Canadian life, to help Canadian institutions adapt to the growing cultural variety within Canadian society and avoid discrimination, and to bring greater national social cohesion and mutual respect. Multiculturalism eliminates racism and racial discrimination, overcomes problems faced by integration, promotes shared national values, and works to build a fair and inclusive society that works for every Canadian.

SEE ALSO:
AFFIRMATIVE ACTION;
CONSTITUTIONAL ACT
OF CANADA.

NAFTA

U.S. President Bill Clinton signs The North American Free Trade Agreement in December 1993.

In 1988, President Ronald Reagan of the United States of America and Prime Minister Brian Mulroney of Canada concluded negotiations on the U.S.-Canada Free Trade Agreement. This set the stage for talks designed to expand regional trade cooperation. After more than a year of negotiations, talks concluded in 1993, and the North American Free Trade Agreement (NAFTA) was drafted.

The three-thousand-page final document, completed November 23, 1993, contains hundreds of regulations designed to create an economic alliance among the three major countries of North America: Canada, the United States, and Mexico. Provisions of NAFTA relating to customs can be found in Title XIX of the United States Code. Sections covering the admission of nonimmigrants are found in Title VIII; those covering inventions made abroad are in Title XXXV, and those concerning court-ordered statements are in Title XLII.

The preamble of NAFTA lists goals that include strengthening the special bonds of friendship and cooperation among the three nations, contributing to the harmonious development and expansion of world trade, creating an expanded and secure market for goods and services produced in the three territories, reducing distortions to trade, enhancing the competitiveness of their firms in global markets, creating new employment opportunities and improving working conditions, strengthening environmental laws and regulations, fostering creativity and innovation, and protecting, enhancing, and enforcing basic workers' rights.

Chapter 1 of NAFTA establishes a free-trade area and it also delineates the objectives of the treaty: eliminating barriers to trade of goods and services, promoting conditions of fair competition, encouraging the development of investment opportunities, protecting and enforcing intellectual property rights, and building a framework for further cooperation that would ultimately enhance the benefits of NAFTA to the countries participating in it.

The treaty set out tariff reductions to be phased in over a ten-to fifteen-year period ending in the mid- to late 1990's on goods that originate in one of the three member nations. Before the implementation of the agreement, Mexican tariffs on imports averaged nearly 11 percent, and similar tariffs

SUMMARY

➤ The 1993 North American Free Trade Agreement (NAFTA) is designed to create an economic alliance among Canada, the United States, and Mexico.
➤ NAFTA reduced trade barriers such as tariffs and quotas to promote the free flow of goods among the three nations.
➤ Supporters said NAFTA would boost stagnating economies, open Mexico's protectionist market, and create high-wage jobs in the United States in electronics.
➤ Opponents feared that many jobs in textile manufacturing and metal production would leave the United States.
➤ Ratification of NAFTA signaled that President William "Bill" Clinton would not follow traditional protectionist policies.

Workers in San Francisco demonstrate prior to the ratification of NAFTA. Many feared it would lead to a loss of jobs in the United States.

averaged 5 percent in Canada and less than 4 percent in the United States. Besides reducing tariffs, NAFTA provides mechanisms to reduce nontariff barriers such as dairy and cotton quotas in the United States and Canada. Ideally, this agreement will encourage investment in all three countries, an idea particularly novel for Mexico, which maintained a ban on outside ownership of certain industries and land areas.

Strict rules of origin were incorporated into the agreement to determine the applicability of the reduced tariff barriers to goods flowing into the United States, Mexico, or Canada. Simply stated, the goods must be wholly obtained or produced in one of the three countries. Further explanation of this rule is in Annex 401.

Supporters touted the treaty as the cure for stagnating economies and claimed that this agreement would open Mexico's protectionist market and create high-wage jobs in the United Staes in areas such as electronics. Opponents countered with claims that tens of thousands of jobs that could not easily be replaced would leave the nation. Endangered industries included textile manufacturing and bulk-metal-production operations.

These initial reservations about the potential loss of jobs within the American market spurred negotiators to establish a multibillion-dollar fund to compensate those Americans whose job loss was directly or indirectly related to the implementation of NAFTA. Additional surge protectors were created in Chapter 8 of the agreement to allow the United States to slow the flow of Mexican goods in the event certain markets become flooded.

The U.S. Congress approved the treaty early in the administration of President Bill Clinton by a 234 to 220 vote (SEE Clinton's Presidency). This legislative victory branded Clinton as a "New Democrat" willing to buck the position of his party to favor the pro-business stance espoused by the Republican Party and the Republican officials who

CAUSES AND EFFECTS

The expansion of the global marketplace over the last half of the twentieth century has given rise to the creation of regional trading blocs. These blocs are organized through treaty arrangements and may prove to be self-sufficient in their ability to support active trading among the member countries. Such blocs include the European Community, nations of the Pacific Rim who are members of the Association of South East Asian Nations (ASEAN), and North American countries operating under NAFTA. The net effect of these regional markets has not yet been determined. Of particular concern will be the effect of these regional agreements on the General Agreement on Tariffs and Trade, commonly known as GATT, and on world trading practices in general.

DAILY LIFE

MAQUILADORAS

A *maquiladora* is an assembly or manufacturing operation located in Mexico near the border with the United States that is partially or wholly owned and managed by non-Mexican persons or entities but uses only Mexican hourly workers. After importing most or all the components from the United States or other nations, these operations use competitively priced Mexican labor to assemble or manufacture goods that may then be exported. As long as the imported components are destined for export within a six-month period, no Mexican import duties are levied. Mexican law also provides for the importation of capital equipment and machinery from abroad for operation in the *maquiladoras*.

Though some *maquiladoras* were operational prior to the ratification of NAFTA, the number has significantly increased since January 1994. Many Fortune 500 companies operate *maquiladoras*, including AT&T, Zenith, Delco, General Electric, Converse, Whirlpool, and TRW. Human-rights violations continue to be of concern to foreign observers. Because the *maquiladoras* typically offer higher wages than other jobs in Mexico, the demand for these positions is high. However, discrimination in employment policies and other workplace abuses are coming to light. The *New York Times* and the Associated Press have reported discrimination against pregnant women in Tijuana *maquiladoras*, in particular, and the exploitation of teenage girls throughout Latin America.

favored passage of this particular treaty. Ratification of NAFTA was seen as a signal that the United States would not drift further in the protectionist direction under Bill Clinton but would expand its role in the global marketplace.

During 1994, trade among NAFTA partners climbed 17 percent. Growth for 1994 was estimated at over $50 billion. U.S. trade with Canada reached $243 billion, and U.S. trade with Mexico rose to over $100 billion for the first time in history. Talks continue surrounding the inclusion of Chile and other Latin American countries. An early objective of the negotiation process was the creation of a Free Trade Area of the Americas by the year 2005.

Donna Addkison Simmons

SEE ALSO:
CLINTON'S PRESIDENCY;
GENERAL AGREEMENT
ON TARIFFS & TRADE;
LABOR MOVEMENT IN
CANADA; LABOR
MOVEMENT IN MEXICO;
LABOR MOVEMENT IN
THE U.S.; LAURIER'S
MINISTRY; MULRONEY'S
MINISTRY; REAGAN'S
PRESIDENCY.

FURTHER READING
• "After NAFTA." *Economist* 326 (March 20, 1993): 20.
• Bandow, Doug, and Ian Vasquez. *Perpetuating Poverty: The World Bank, the IMF, and the Developing World.* Washington, D.C.: Cato Institute, 1994.
• Bryan, Lowell L. *Market Unbound: Unleashing Global Capitalism.* New York: John Wiley & Sons, 1996.
• Kennaj, M., and R. Florida. "Japanese *Maquiladoras*: Production Organization and Global Commodity Chains." *World Development* 22 (January, 1994): 27-44.
• "More Muck than Money." *Economist* 329 (October 16, 1993): 50.
• Naisbitt, John. *Global Paradox: The Bigger the World Economy, the More Powerful Its Smallest Players.* New York: William Morrow, 1994.
• Rohwer, Jim. *Asia Rising.* New York: Simon & Schuster, 1995.

William Bywater, president of the electrical workers' union, makes a speech in 1993 opposing the North American Free Trade Agreement.

Narváez & Cabeza de Vaca

Álvar Núñez Cabeza de Vaca left Spain in 1527 to act as royal treasurer for Pánfilo de Narváez' expedition to Florida.

SUMMARY

➤ Álvar Núñez Cabeza de Vaca accompanied Pánfilo de Narváez on a disastrous expedition to Florida in 1527.
➤ Six hundred people began the trip, and only four reached New Spain.
➤ In April, 1528, Narváez' land party lost contact with his ships, which returned to New Spain.
➤ The explorers, diminished by exhaustion, illness, and hostile Indians, attempted to sail west to New Spain, but many died at sea, and those who landed in present-day eastern Texas were made slaves of the Indians.
➤ Cabeza de Vaca and three others who survived traveled west over land, finally reaching Culiacán in 1536.

Many of the Spanish conquerors and explorers of the Western Hemisphere wrote chronicles, which were a traditional genre in Spanish literature. Though few were learned scholars or creators of beauty, their chronicles are filled with creative power as well as valuable historical information.

Among these men was Álvar Núñez Cabeza de Vaca, the first Spaniard to traverse, on foot, a large portion of the recently discovered territory of North America. The journey of Cabeza de Vaca (1528–1536) predates the expeditions of Hernando de Soto and Francisco Vásquez de Coronado in what later became the United States of America (SEE Coronado's Expediton; De Soto's Expedition). Cabeza de Vaca's odyssey of hardship and misfortune is one of the most remarkable in the history of the New World.

A product of Cabeza de Vaca's journey was *La Relación* (the account), first published in Zamora, Spain, in 1542, with a second edition published in Valladolid, Spain, in 1555. Cabeza de Vaca's chronicle is one of the earliest accounts of Spanish penetration in North America. *La Relación* contains many first descriptions of the lands and their inhabitants and is one of the first Spanish accounts that calls for a compassionate and tolerant policy toward the natives of the Western Hemisphere.

Cabeza de Vaca was born around 1490 in Jerez de la Frontera, an Andalusian town famous for its sherry. He was the fourth son of Francisco de Vera, an alderman of Jerez, and Teresa Cabeza de Vaca. After spending his youth in Jerez de la Frontera, Cabeza de Vaca entered military service.

THE EXPEDITION BEGINS

On February 15, 1527, Cabeza de Vaca was appointed royal treasurer of Pánfilo de Narváez' expedition to Florida, one of the most disastrous enterprises in the annals of Spanish history. Governor Pánfilo de Narváez' expedition set out from Spain on June 17, 1527, to conquer and govern "the provinces that lie on the mainland from the River of Palms to Cape Florida" by the king's authority and orders. It consisted of five ships and crews totaling about six hundred men.

After sailing from Sanlúcar Barrameda, the ships stopped in the Canary Islands, then sailed for almost three months until they reached Hispaniola in mid-August. They replenished their supplies on the island of Hispaniola, and Narváez attempted, without success, to recruit additional crew members.

From Hispaniola, they went to Cuba, where they spent the winter of 1527–1528 but experienced setbacks. After many days in Santiago de Cuba and Trinidad, they gradually acquired the provisions the expedition needed to continue on its way.

The cost of the expedition was borne by Narváez and the wealthy Spaniard Vasco Porcallo de Figueroa, who was living in Cuba and years later joined Hernando de Soto's expedition. Cabeza de Vaca stayed with some of the crew in the Bay of Jagua at the entrance of Cienfuegos, while Narváez stayed in the Bay of Santa Cruz.

They at last set foot in Florida on April 14, 1528, in a coastal area near Tampa Bay, perhaps very near Boca Ciega. Following a dispute between Cabeza de Vaca and Narváez, a party of about three hundred men led by Narváez struck out into the peninsula. They briefly marched east and later north on a route parallel to the Florida coast, through a region that abounded in swamps, poisonous snakes, and harsh and noxious vegetation. Narváez had left a hundred men with the

ships, which were to sail along the coast and eventually meet up with the main group. However, these crews, guided by an inexperienced captain, lost contact with the land party in a matter of days. In the end, the ships returned to New Spain (present-day Mexico and Central America) after giving up Narváez' group for lost.

By the time Narváez' group reached the northernmost part of Florida, near the city of Tallahassee, it had been diminished by exhaustion, illness, and the often-savage battles with American Indians (SEE Southeastern American Indians). Very near a village occupied by the Apalachee tribe,

Santiago de Cuba, one of the places where Narváez and Cabeza de Vaca acquired provisions for their expedition during the winter of 1527–1528.

Narváez faced hazardous terrain filled with swamps and deadly snakes after the expedition landed near Tampa Bay in Florida on April 14, 1528.

which the Spaniards called the Aute, the survivors of the expedition decided to construct boats and sail westward, following the coast that was their only guide. They believed that the route would take them to already explored and conquered regions of New Spain.

DISASTER AND A LONG TREK

The attempt to travel in small flatboats turned into a disaster. Many crewmen were killed, and the rest were stranded on the coast of present-day eastern Texas. By the autumn of 1528, Cabeza de Vaca and his companions were left defenseless and destitute among groups of Karankawa Indians who lived on these coasts.

They did not imagine that they would spend years of slavery and indescribable suffering in this desolate region, years that would kill all but four of the three hundred men who had landed in Florida: Andrés Dorantes de Carranza, Alonso del Castillo Maldonado, the Moroccan slave Estevanico (Estevan), and Cabeza de Vaca. A Greek named Teodoro may have survived by joining Indian tribes in that region. Information collected years later by

DAILY LIFE

LIFE AT SEA

While Pánfilo de Narváez' expedition was in Florida, the group became disheartened by the death of many soldiers and other misfortunes. The group decided to escape by making flatboats and sailing west to New Spain. However, traversing the Gulf of Mexico in small, open boats proved disastrous. Many, including Narváez, were swept out to sea and lost. Others in the group, among them Álvar Núñez Cabeza de Vaca, managed to land on the coast of present-day Texas, where they were enslaved by Indians.

Narváez' expedition was fraught with disaster from the moment it first sighted land in the New World. Two of the five ships, along with all on board, sank during a hurricane in Santo Domingo. The remaining vessels were beset by three more storms before they finally reached Tampa Bay, Florida, with very little food and most of their horses dead and the rest unfit for service. Narváez separated his expedition in two parties.

Three hundred men proceeded up the coast on foot, and the rest were to sail alongside it. After six weeks of arduous exploration and dwindling hope of meeting the ships, the land party decided to construct the flatboats. On September 22, 1528, they set sail for the port of Panuco, New Spain, in five flatboats.

After thirty days of suffering, during which several men died, the boats were separated by a storm, and all five eventually were beached by another storm off the coast of present-day Texas. Two boats, one of which carried Cabeza de Vaca, landed on the coast of Galveston Island. Two others, one of them commanded by Narváez, were carried out to sea by a high wind and never seen again. The fifth craft had landed still farther down the coast, but the men were so weak that they were unable to offer any resistance, and the Indians killed all of them.

CAUSES AND EFFECTS

The Spaniards attributed anything positive that happened to them to divine mercy and goodness. Through his writings, Álvar Núñez Cabeza de Vaca demonstrates this faith. His chronicle radiates a spiritual quality and is concerned with ultimates and with people's relationships to God, to the universe, and to their own souls. Cabeza de Vaca's journey revealed, among other things, the vast extent of territory between the two oceans and the existence of an unknown land mass of continental proportions north of New Spain.

Previously North America had been believed to be quite narrow, and apparently the truth did not sink into the understanding of English geographers for a century or more after it became common knowledge in Spain. The mention of two advanced Native American cultures and the possible riches of North America promoted subsequent journeys of conquest and exploration.

Hernando de Soto's men suggests that Teodoro was sacrificed by the Indians.

After long delays and detours, Cabeza de Vaca and his companions journeyed toward the west, pausing at times with clans and tribes of Coahuiltec, Jumano, Opata, Pima, and other Indians (SEE Southwestern American Indians). During their long pilgrimage, Cabeza de Vaca and his companions had to survive under conditions of desperate need and played the part of medicine men more than once.

Always traveling westward, and later toward the south, Cabeza de Vaca and his men finally met a group of Spanish soldiers who were laying siege to native communities in northern New Spain (SEE Spanish Conquest). The long-desired encounter took place after eight years of wandering through deserts and inhospitable regions, amid inclement weather conditions, often naked and totally without protection.

However, Cabeza de Vaca says almost nothing about the joy and rejoicing that resulted from meeting fellow countrymen. Cabeza de Vaca and his companions at last reached the village of Culiacán on April 1, 1536. Castillo, Dorantes, and Estevanico stayed in New Spain.

Cabeza de Vaca began his return journey to Spain from Veracruz on April 10, 1537, and disembarked in Lisbon, Portugal, on August 9, 1537. Cabeza de Vaca would later return to the Americas, but this time to the regions of Río de la Plata in South America, in command of three ships and with the rank of governor.

Juana Iris Goergen

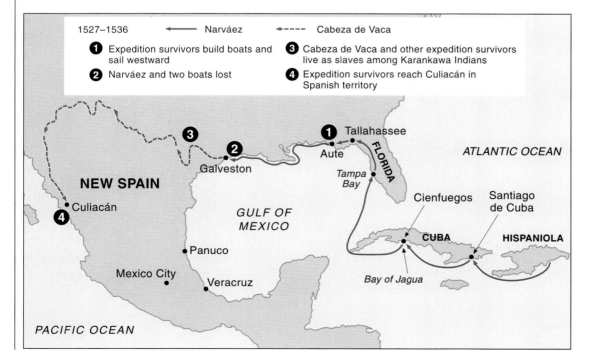

1527–1536   ⟵ Narváez   ⟵---- Cabeza de Vaca

1 Expedition survivors build boats and sail westward

2 Narváez and two boats lost

3 Cabeza de Vaca and other expedition survivors live as slaves among Karankawa Indians

4 Expedition survivors reach Culiacán in Spanish territory

The expedition made by Narváez and Cabeza de Vaca from 1527 to 1536 aimed to conquer and govern new territories in North America for the Spanish crown.

FURTHER READING

•Adorno, Rolena. "The Negotiation of Fear in Cabeza de Vaca's *Naufragios*." *Representations* 33 (1991): 163–199.

•Cabeza de Vaca, Álvar Núñez. *The Account: Álvar Núñez Cabeza de Vaca's Relación*. Translated by Martin A. Favata and José B. Fernández. Houston, Texas: Arte Público Press, 1993.

•_____. *Castaways*. Edited by Enrique Pupo-Walker. Translated by Frances M. López-Morillas. Berkeley: University of California Press, 1993.

•Marrinan, Rochelle A., John F. Scarry, and Rhonda L. Majors. "Prelude to De Soto: The Expedition of Pánfilo de Narváez." In *Columbian Consequences*, edited by David Hurst Thomas. Vol. 2. Washington, D.C.: Smithsonian Institution Press, 1990.

•Paisley, Clifton. *The Red Hills of Florida, 1528–1865*. Tuscaloosa: University of Alabama Press, 1989.

•Terrell, John Upton. *Estevanico the Black*. Los Angeles: Westernlore, 1968.

PROFILE

ESTEVANICO (DIED 1539)

Estevanico, also known as Estevan, was the Moorish slave of Andrés Dorantes de Carranza, a captain on the expedition led by Pánfilo de Narváez. In his chronicle, Álvar Núñez Cabeza de Vaca refers to Estevanico as "El Negro," or the black one, until November 1532 when the American Indians tell Cabeza de Vaca about bearded men like him who were in that vicinity. He found them to be two of Narváez' captains, Dorantes and Alonso del Castillo Maldonaldo, who are with Estevanico.

Soon after Cabeza de Vaca and the others arrived in New Spain, Estevanico, who spoke six native languages, was borrowed or purchased from Dorantes by Antonio de Mendoza, viceroy of New Spain, to act as a guide to Fray Marcos de Niza on a journey northward in search of the mythical Seven Cities of Cíbola.

Marcos' expedition left Culiacán on March 7, 1539. Upon reaching the native village of Vacapa, Fray Marcos stopped and sent Estevanico on ahead with orders to halt at once and return himself or send back messengers if he found something wonderful. Because Estevanico could neither read nor write, Fray Marcos instructed him to send back a cross the size of one hand if he learned of anything of "medium importance," the size of two hands if he learned of something of great importance, and a still larger cross if he learned of a country "bigger and better than New Spain."

Four days after Estevanico's departure, Fray Marcos received a cross "the size of a man," along with a message urging him to hurry on because "the greatest country in the world" lay ahead. Shortly thereafter, Estevanico sent a second large cross and, disregarding instructions, was speeding on and sending back message after message for the friar to hurry. Fray Marcos, however, who was advanced in years and in poor health, moved ahead slowly. Within one day's march of Cíbola, he met three of the Indians who had accompanied Estevanico. They told him that Estevanico, upon reaching Cíbola, had incurred the wrath of the Cíbolans, and he and his company had been seized, imprisoned overnight, and all but the three of them had been slain the next morning. Estevanico died at Hawikuh, New Mexico, in 1539.

This Zuñi pueblo in present-day Arizona was supposedly one of the Seven Cities of Cíbola. Estevanico was a guide for Fray Marcos de Niza in his search for the mythical cities in 1533.

National Organization for Women

The National Organization for Women (NOW), established in 1966, is dedicated to economic, political, and social gender equality.

During the 1970's, NOW focused its efforts on ratification of the Equal Rights Amendment (ERA), which stated "Equality of rights under the law shall not be denied or abridged by the United States or by any State on account of sex." ERA proponents achieved several early victories in the struggle for ratification of the amendment, but a powerful anti-ERA coalition that was led by the conservative Phyllis Schlafly emerged, and despite receiving support from Presidents Gerald Ford and Jimmy Carter, the ERA failed to secure the approval of three-fourths of the states.

After the ERA was defeated in 1982, NOW became increasingly active in the internal politics of the Democratic Party. During the early 1970's, the McGovern-Fraser Commission had called on the party to develop its goals for increased female representation at its nominating conventions. Later commissions established the standard for equal gender representation at Democratic conventions.

In 1984, NOW and other feminist organizations used their political strength to support the candidacy of Walter Mondale. NOW lobbied on behalf of a female vice presidential nominee, and Mondale named Representative Geraldine Ferraro of New York his running mate.

NOW has proven an effective voice for equal rights for women, although its failure to organize a larger percentage of American females has hampered its success. The organization's agenda, liberal in ideological terms, places it at a disadvantage in terms of fulfilling the role of an ideologically diverse interest group.

As a result, NOW has been joined by a host of other women's groups, conservative and liberal, that give voice to those diverse views. NOW was simply one of the first, and it was one of the most active.

Michael E. Meagher

Betty Friedan founded the National Organization for Women in 1966.

CAUSES AND EFFECTS

Betty Friedan, the author of the influential *The Feminine Mystique*, was instrumental in founding the National Organization for Women and served as its first president. NOW pledged "to take action to bring women into full participation in the mainstream of American society now, exercising all the privileges and responsibilities thereof in truly equal partnership with men." Friedan's book appeared at a time when women's issues were becoming increasingly visible. The Kennedy Commission on the Status of Women (1963), a study of discriminatory practices against women, was followed by legislative victories.

In addition to passing an Equal Pay Act in 1963, Congress included an amendment against sexual discrimination in the 1964 Civil Rights Act. However, these provisions were not enforced, causing advocates of gender equality to support the establishment of a feminist interest group.

SEE ALSO: CARTER'S PRESIDENCY; CIVIL RIGHTS ACT OF 1964; EQUAL PAY ACT; KENNEDY'S PRESIDENCY; WOMEN'S RIGHTS MOVEMENT.

National Park Service

The traditional arrowhead emblem of the U.S. National Park Service, which greets visitors at the entrance to its parks.

SUMMARY

➤ Congress established the National Park Service in 1916 to manage and promote national parks, monuments, and reservations.
➤ Stephen Mather, the first director, made the parks more accessible to visitors.
➤ In the 1920's and 1930's, public and private organizations worked with officials to buy land and relocate residents so that parks could be created in the eastern United States.
➤ In 1933, additional monuments, historic sites and buildings, and national military parks were placed under the control of the Park Service.
➤ Over the years, the Park Service has faced the problem of encouraging park use while protecting valuable resources.

The National Park Service was established by the U.S. Congress on August 25, 1916, to manage and promote federal areas known as national parks, monuments, and reservations. A number of national parks, including Yellowstone National Park (first established in 1872), Grand Canyon, Yosemite, Crater Lake, and Mount Rainier, were created, primarily, to protect unique geological features. Even after land had been set aside, however, debate continued about how to use the national parks. Some people wanted national parks to be enjoyed as they were and left unchanged for future generations. Others wanted to manage wilderness and other public lands scientifically and for practical purposes. Still others looked to the national parks for economic gain.

In the beginning, Congress saw the parks as areas that would require no federal money

and be self-supporting. It provided very little funding, and the parks were sparsely staffed. However, by 1916, Congress had decided to give the national parks more political standing through the formal establishment of the National Park Service in the Department of the Interior. The untitled August 25 act, commonly known as the National Park Service Act or Organic Act, stated that the Park Service was to "conserve the scenery and the natural and historic objects and wild life therein, and to provide for the enjoyment of the same in such manner and by such means as will leave them unimpaired for the enjoyment of future generations."

The first director, Stephen Mather, worked hard to make the Park Service a professional organization and a large and influential part of Washington's bureaucracy. He wanted the parks to serve as sources of education. He had Park Service rangers provide information and help visitors understand and appreciate nature. Mather encouraged tourism, recognizing that the more people visited the park, the more money Congress would appropriate. He worked with railroads to provide transportation and accommodations. Although he valued preservation, he fostered recreational facilities such as swimming pools, golf courses, and tennis courts that in later years would not be considered appropriate for the parks.

Mather realized that the park system would not be truly national until parks were located throughout the country, not confined to the West. His belief had a pragmatic side to it: Most of the nation's population and the monetary support for the federal government were in the East. Problems arose because the major reason for establishing parks in the West was to enshrine spectacular geological features. Fewer monumental features existed in the East, so some had to be "manufactured." The Appalachian Mountains were seen as a possible location for an Eastern park, but people lived in the sections that were particularly attractive. In the 1920's and 1930's, public and private organizations

CAUSES AND EFFECTS

In the late 1800's, national parks had little political clout and thus were not seen as important or deserving of respect or federal funds. Years of campaigning by men such as Secretaries of the Interior Richard Ballinger, Walter Fisher, and Franklin Lane; American Civic Association president J. Horace McFarland; Representative William Kent; Senator Reed Smoot; and landscape architect and conservationist Frederick Law Olmsted, Jr., helped convince Congress of the value of a new agency to manage and promote the parks. With the passage of the national Park Service Act in 1916, more national parks were established and were no longer located only in the West. Official recognition of the importance of preservation increased.

worked with local, state, and federal officials to raise money to buy the land and move the residents. In this manner, the national parks of the Great Smoky Mountains on the border of Kentucky and Tennessee, Shenandoah in Virginia, Acadia in Maine, Mammoth Cave in Kentucky, and Hot Springs in Arkansas were established.

The facilities in the Eastern parks had been constructed largely through the work of the Civilian Conservation Corps. The corps also helped to build facilities and roads in already existing parks. These construction

The national parks of the United States, which are spread across the country, feature some of the most spectacular secenery in North America.

PROFILE

JOHN MUIR (1838–1914)

John Muir was born in Dunbar, Scotland, on April 21, 1838. He lived in Wisconsin and moved to California in 1868. As a transcendentalist, he wrote extensively about the spiritual value of nature. He worked hard for wilderness preservation and was the founder and first president of the Sierra Club (1892), which is devoted to nature preservation. He worked with Robert Underwood Anderson of *Century Magazine* to convince Congress to establish Yosemite National Park, which it did, in 1890. In 1906, the state park inside Yosemite became part of the national park. However, Muir lost a thirteen-year battle over the flooding of the beautiful Hetch Hetchy Valley in the park when in 1913 Congress authorized the damming of the Tuolumne River to provide San Francisco with water.

Muir's efforts helped create national preserves in Rainier, the Grand Canyon, the Petrified Forest, and parts of the Sierra. He published several books, including *Our National Parks* (1901), in which he presented arguments for conservation and ecological protection. He spent his last years traveling through Europe, South America, and Africa. Muir, who died in Los Angeles in 1914, provided the foundation for later conservation and ecology movements.

John Muir (right) with Theodore Roosevelt on a mountaintop above Yosemite Valley. Roosevelt exhibited a keen interest in nature and conservation.

SEE ALSO:
GRANT'S PRESIDENCY;
ROOSEVELT'S
(FRANKLIN D.)
PRESIDENCY; ROOSEVELT'S
(THEODORE) PRESIDENCY;
WILSON'S PRESIDENCY

FURTHER READING
•Frome, M., R. W. Waver, and P. Pritchard. "United States: National Parks." In *International Handbook of National Parks and Nature Reserves*, edited by Craig W. Allin. New York: Greenwood Press, 1990.
•Ise, John. *Our National Park Policy: A Critical History*. Baltimore: The Johns Hopkins University Press, 1961.
•Ridenour, James. *The National Parks Compromised: Pork Barrel Politics and America's Treasures*. Merrillville, Ind.: ICS Books, 1994.
•Runte, Alfred. *National Parks: The American Experience*. 3d ed. Lincoln: University of Nebraska Press, 1997.

projects, though beneficial overall, may have inhibited preservation in the parks by opening up some previously inaccessible wilderness areas.

In 1933, the federal government expanded the role of the National Park Service to include certain national lands that had been under the control of the Departments of War and Agriculture, including monuments, historic sites and buildings, and national military parks. This transfer of twelve natural areas in nine Western states and fifty-seven historical areas in seventeen Eastern states gave the National Park Service and its parent agency, the Department of the Interior, significantly increased political clout. The operations of the Park Service were now more broadly distributed throughout the country. By preserving and managing important historical sites along with natural ones, the Park Service was enlarging its role and more completely fulfilling the mission set out in 1916.

The types of problems that affected the parks' development in their first years of existence continued, sometimes with more intensity. Congress still had difficulty in justifying the value of setting aside land for the sole purpose of preservation and not permitting any exploitation of resources. Other problems involved the constant attacks on the parks and their resources by wide-ranging private and public interests.

The parks originally contained lands valued for their scenic wonders. Over the decades, the Park Service has expanded the types of areas it manages and refers to them as park units. Historic sites and parks, memorial parks, battlefield parks and sites, lakeshores, seashores, monuments, parkways, scenic trails, scenic rivers and riverways, capital parks, and recreation areas fall within the Park Service purview. As a result, more and more people are using and enjoying areas administered by the Park Service. Overuse, however, creates its own serious problems: congestion, pollution, and in some cases destruction. The Park Service continues to face the problem of simultaneously encouraging use and protecting valuable national resources so that they remain unimpaired for future generations.

Margaret F. Boorstein

National Security Act

After a long military and political debate, the National Security Act of 1947 emerged as the first major attempt to develop a modern organizational structure for the U.S. military establishment. It created three nonmilitary agencies—National Security Council, Central Intelligence Agency, and National Security Resources Board—to coordinate national security. The National Security Council would be chaired by the president and include as permanent members the secretaries of state, defense, army, navy, air force and the chairman of the National Security Resources Board. Other members could be added if circumstances dictated.

The council would advise the president on national security matters. The Central Intelligence Agency would provide the best possible intelligence to enable the council to make informed policy decisions. The National Security Resource Board would provide advice on the "coordination of military, industrial, and civilian mobilization." The national military establishment would be led by the secretary of defense, who was the principal assistant to the president on national security issues. However, the act created three separate departments (Army, Navy, and Air Force), whose secretaries sat on the president's cabinet and the National Security Council. This made it difficult if not impossible for the secretary of defense to coordinate the military departments, which could take their cases directly to the president and the Congress. The Department of Defense also oversaw the Joint Chiefs of Staff, a munitions board, and a resource and development board. President Harry S. Truman appointed James Forrestal, who had been instrumental in the development of the act, as the first secretary of defense.

Robert Franklin Maddox

CAUSES AND EFFECTS

In November 1943 General George C. Marshall, Army chief of staff, proposed the establishment of a post-World War II unified military department. The reasons for it included the growing complexity of the office of president, U.S. leadership in the Cold War, the military science and technology revolution, the need for coordinated intelligence, the success of the combined operations during World War II, and the postwar pressure to cut spending. Unfortunately the unification legislation failed to put an end to the bickering among the service branches, failing to provide the defense secretary sufficient authority to enforce cooperation. Ultimately, Congress gave more authority to the defense secretary in amendments to the original legislation in 1949.

SEE ALSO:
COLD WAR; TRUMAN'S
PRESIDENCY.

Navajos' "Long Walk"

CAUSES AND EFFECTS

The westward expansion of the United States collided with Navajo culture and traditions. In an attempt to end Navajo raiding and to assimilate them into Euro-American life, General James Carleton removed them from their ancestral homelands.

The removal of the Navajo to Bosque Redondo, a reservation in eastern New Mexico, did not result in their total assimilation. The Navajo did, however, give up their traditional practice of raiding.

Their experiences during the Long Walk united the Navajo, laying the groundwork for the creation of the Navajo Nation.

SEE ALSO:
CIVIL WAR; NEZ
PERCE EXILE;
SOUTHWESTERN
AMERICAN INDIANS;
WESTWARD EXPANSION.

Kit Carson, the frontiersman, inflicted terrible damage on the Navajo, forcing them on the Long Walk away from their homeland.

During the mid-1860's, the United States Army forcefully removed more than eight thousand Navajo from their northeastern Arizona and northwestern New Mexico homelands. In what is known as the Long Walk, the Navajo marched 300 miles (483 kilometers) to Bosque Redondo, a reservation in eastern New Mexico. Brigadier General James Carleton, the military commander of New Mexico Territory, designed this policy to assimilate the Navajo into Euro-American life.

The Navajo were skilled raiders, and they practiced their trade throughout the Southwest. During the Civil War, they expanded their raiding range by looting American and Mexican settlements. Carleton devised a plan to bring an end to Navajo raids and open Navajo lands to settlement and mining (SEE Westward Expansion). He ordered Colonel Christopher "Kit" Carson to pursue and destroy all Navajo who would not surrender and go to Bosque Redondo.

Throughout the winter of 1863–1864, Carson marched through Dinetah, the Navajo homeland, destroying crops, killing livestock, and chopping down peach orchards. This harsh military campaign resulted in the surrender of most Navajo.

The Navajo traveled to Bosque Redondo in several waves. In February and March 1864, troops escorted more than 4,000 Navajo to their new home. By December 31, 1864, a total of 8,354 Navajo had walked to Bosque Redondo. Almost 2,000 Navajo, however, never surrendered and remained in the mountainous regions of Dinetah. The Navajo faced many dangers on the Long Walk. Many died from dysentery, malnutrition, and exposure. Others were kidnapped and enslaved by whites, Mexicans, and other American Indians. Perhaps 10 percent of the Navajo who began the Long Walk never arrived at Bosque Redondo.

Miserable living conditions and incompetent administration at Bosque Redondo doomed Carleton's plan to resettle and assimilate the Navajo. The reservation was too small to sustain the Navajo. Crop failures, insect infestations, drought, poor land, unscrupulous traders, and Comanche raids made life at Bosque Redondo unbearable. Many Navajo abandoned the reservation and moved back to their homeland. Finally, Secretary of War Edwin Stanton relieved Carleton of his command on September 19, 1866. The government negotiated a treaty with the Navajo that established a reservation on a portion of their homeland. On June 18, 1868, under escort of federal troops, the Navajo began their long walk home.

Mark R. Ellis

New Deal

The Grand Coulee Dam on the Columbia River, Washington State, was completed in 1941. Its construction was part of President Franklin D. Roosevelt's New Deal for national economic recovery.

The U.S. presidential campaign of 1932 centered on the Great Depression. After the stock market crash in October 1929, thousands of businesses and banks folded, farms and small businesses went bankrupt, and the number of unemployed Americans quadrupled. Voters lost faith in President Herbert Hoover's ability to end the Depression (SEE Hoover's Presidency). The Democratic challenger, Franklin D. Roosevelt, promised "a new deal for the American people." Roosevelt easily won the presidency, but he still had no concrete plan for ending the Depression. He believed that through experimentation he could find an answer (SEE Roosevelt's Presidency).

THE FIRST NEW DEAL

The First New Deal measures began in 1933 and continued to mid-1934. In Roosevelt's first hundred days in office (March 9–June 16, 1933), Congress enacted more than a dozen measures that offered relief to banking, agriculture, industry, and the unemployed. First addressing the banking crisis, Roosevelt bought time by declaring a four-day bank holiday. Following the holiday, banks could reopen under increased federal regulation and with a Treasury Department license. In June 1933 an act of Congress created the Federal Deposit Insurance Corporation (FDIC), which insured personal bank deposits for up to $5,000.

The early New Deal also targeted farm relief. Roosevelt believed that limiting the production of certain crops and livestock would lead to higher market prices for farmers. Therefore, a federal agency paid farmers to reduce their production.

Having already planted crops in the spring of 1933, many farmers were thus paid to plow crops under and slaughter millions of piglets and pregnant sows. This act was unpopular with most Americans, who could not understand the destruction of food when so many were starving. Additionally, the federal payments rarely reached the poorest farmers: sharecroppers, tenants, migrant workers, and farm laborers.

Roosevelt also made some attempts to provide relief for industries and unemployed workers. Under the National Recovery

SUMMARY

➤ From 1933 to 1939, U.S. president Franklin D. Roosevelt focused his domestic policy on ending the Great Depression.
➤ His program for doing so, called the New Deal, involved greater government participation in the nation's economy.
➤ Roosevelt's legislation sought to aid farmers and workers and to stabilize banking and investment.
➤ The Supreme Court, conservative at the time, struck down some of Roosevelt's measures.
➤ Although Roosevelt was concerned about deficit spending and tried to limit it, his social welfare programs entailed deficit spending.
➤ Some New Deal programs, such as the National Recovery Administration, failed, but others, such as Social Security and the Federal Deposit Insurance Corporation, were enduring successes.

CAUSES AND EFFECTS

On October 29, 1929, the stock market crashed and sent the economy spiraling downward over the next four years. Income levels fell drastically, banks failed, businesses and farms went bankrupt, and unemployment soared. Many Americans voted for Franklin D. Roosevelt in 1932 hoping he could pull the nation out of the Great Depression. Roosevelt's solution was the New Deal. Even after some of the New Deal programs were enacted, other events, such as the Dust Bowl and occasionally decreased federal spending, prolonged the Depression. The New Deal did not end the Great Depression.

Even though the New Deal did not emphasize racial equality, some programs did benefit African-Americans. Roosevelt's New Deal also led to a political coalition for the Democratic Party that kept a Democrat in the White House until the 1950's. The New Deal increased the power of the presidency as Roosevelt took control of the nation's economic crisis. With the New Deal, the federal government assumed a much larger role in the lives of ordinary Americans. In addition, the government became more responsive to interest groups other than big business. Finally, Roosevelt pushed through measures that provided a regulatory and social service package to prevent future depressions.

In the 1930's President Franklin D. Roosevelt created the idea of the New Deal for the United States and quickly put it into action.

Administration (NRA), business leaders within each industry regulated themselves by devising their own codes to ensure fair competition. Recognizing the workers' right to bargain with their employers, the NRA also benefited organized labor. Roosevelt hoped the NRA would stimulate production and get the unemployed back to work. Other New Deal measures provided relief in the form of jobs for thousands of unemployed Americans. Government-sponsored projects included reforestation and construction of roads, bridges, dams, and buildings. In addition to jobs, the Tennessee Valley Authority (TVA) also brought hydroelectric power, flood control, recreational facilities, and a soil conservation system to one of the nation's poorest regions. The First New Deal increased federal control over the stock market. Congress passed the Federal Securities Act to regulate the sale of stocks. A year later Congress created the Securities and Exchange Commission (SEC), an agency to supervise the stock market.

SETBACKS

Despite Roosevelt's New Deal, the Depression lingered into 1934. Although the economy was improving, unemployment and national income still remained far below their pre-Depression levels. As the Depression continued, Roosevelt faced a challenge from the Supreme Court, which included several justices who staunchly opposed the New Deal. The Court ruled, in 1935 and 1936, respectively, that the NRA and the Agricultural Adjustment Act (AAA) were unconstitutional.

Roosevelt also became concerned with federal spending. In the first hundred days, the president authorized massive spending to relieve people suffering from the Depression. He intended for the increased spending to be temporary. In 1934 Roosevelt tried to cut back on the federal government's deficit spending. After the winter of 1933–1934, the

Father Charles E. Coughlin, a radical Roman Catholic priest, initially admired Roosevelt's New Deal but later mounted furious attacks against it.

president abolished an agency that had provided jobs.

THE SECOND NEW DEAL

The Second New Deal began after the 1934 midterm elections, in which Democrats enjoyed a large majority in Congress. Seeing the Democratic victory as approval of his New Deal programs, Roosevelt turned to measures that focused less on relief and more on recovery and reform. These initiatives targeted the jobless, the rural poor, organized labor, and the elderly and increased regulation of business and taxes on the wealthy.

TURNING POINT

THE HUNDRED DAYS

In a flurry of activity and experimentation, Roosevelt offered more than a dozen important pieces of legislation between March 6 and June 16, 1933, attempting to relieve the suffering of various groups of Americans. The Emergency Banking Act and the Federal Deposit Insurance Corporation targeted banks. The Agricultural Adjustment Act tried to help farmers.

The National Industrial Recovery Act, the National Recovery Administration, and the Public Works Administration focused on aiding business and labor. Other measures, such as the Federal Emergency Relief Act, the Tennessee Valley Authority, and the Civilian Conservation Corps, emphasized economic development and employment.

After the Supreme Court ruled the AAA unconstitutional in 1936, Congress set up another program that also paid farmers to cut production as well as plant soil-enriching grasses. After the Supreme Court ruled the NRA unconstitutional, Roosevelt pushed through the National Labor Relations Act which, like the NRA, aided laborers. This prounion act guaranteed the workers' right to collective bargaining and encouraged many workers to join unions.

One of the longest-lasting measures of the New Deal, the Social Security Act of 1935, was aimed at older Americans (SEE Social Security Act). This act called for employees to put aside a small fraction of their incomes during each pay period and for employers to contribute as well. This fund would then provide an old-age pension for workers, benefits for survivors of industrial accidents, unemployment insurance, and aid for dependent mothers and children, the blind, and people with disabilities. At the time the effects of the measure were limited. Benefit payments were low and excluded farmers, domestic workers, and the self-employed. Significantly, it established a precedent for the federal government to be responsible for social welfare.

COURT PACKING

In 1936, Roosevelt easily won reelection. Many voters from the groups his measures aided, such as farmers, union workers, and African-Americans, switched to the Democratic Party. With an even stronger mandate than that of the 1932 election, the president attempted to defeat the New Deal's strongest opposition, the Supreme Court. In February 1937 the president devised a court reform bill that would allow him to diminish the power of the judges then sitting on the Supreme Court. The bill allowed the president to appoint a new judge to a bench on which a judge older than seventy sat. While the president claimed that he was worried about the health and workload of the current justices, many of whom were older than seventy, his political motivations were clear to everyone. Roosevelt found himself facing opposition not only from his traditional political enemies but also from many of his

A worker confers with an official at a field office of the Works Progress Administration, a government agency that was set up under the New Deal to help the unemployed.

This later New Deal took shape as Roosevelt anticipated the presidential election of 1936. Three people in particular, Father Charles E. Coughlin in Detroit, Frances Townshend in California, and Huey P. Long in Louisiana, criticized the president for not redistributing the wealth to benefit the poorest Americans. Unemployment, low income, and labor strikes led Roosevelt to respond with reforms.

Not wanting people to become dependent on government handouts, the Works Progress Administration (WPA) required its recipients to work on federal projects. This led to the Federal Writers' Project, which provided opportunities for authors to write state histories and guides and for many others to interview former slaves and record their experiences. In an effort to aid the rural poor, Congress set up an agency to make it easier for small farmers to buy their own farms through loans. In 1935, the Rural Electrification Administration provided loans for utility companies and cooperatives that brought electricity to many rural areas.

LAWS AND CASES

BLACK MONDAY

In 1934 two of Roosevelt's New Deal programs, the National Recovery Act (NRA) and the Agricultural Adjustment Act (AAA), increasingly came under attack. Leaders in big business complained that the NRA involved too much federal regulation. In contrast, small business owners thought it favored large businesses. Many industry leaders began drafting trivial codes for their industry that had no bearing on economic growth. Furthermore, Republicans and several Supreme Court justices believed the NRA was unconstitutional.

On May 27, 1935, Black Monday, the Court declared three New Deal measures, including the NRA, unconstitutional. Even though the day that the Supreme Court defeated Roosevelt was known as Black Monday, the loss of the NRA was not significant. New Dealers realized that the NRA had already failed because it was not stimulating economic growth. Still, the Court's action set a precedent for the judicial branch overthrowing New Deal measures. In 1936 the Supreme Court declared the AAA unconstitutional. In both cases, Roosevelt and his congressional supporters later drafted and passed measures similar to those struck down to achieve the initial goals of economic expansion and aid to farmers.

The blue eagle symbol of the National Recovery Administration was displayed on shop windows and on advertisements between 1933 and 1935.

SEE ALSO: CONSTITUTION OF THE U.S.; DEMOCRATIC PARTY; DUST BOWL; FAIR LABOR STANDARDS ACT; GREAT DEPRESSION; HOOVER'S PRESIDENCY; PROHIBITION; ROOSEVELT'S (FRANKLIN D.) PRESIDENCY; SOCIAL SECURITY ACT; WORKS PROGRESS ADMINISTRATION.

FURTHER READING

• Conkin, Paul K. *The New Deal*. 3d ed. Arlington Heights, Ill.: Harlan Davidson, 1992.

• Leuchtenburg, William E. *Franklin D. Roosevelt and the New Deal, 1932–1940*. New York: Harper Torchbooks, 1963.

• Patterson, James T. *The New Deal and the States: Federalism in Transition*. Princeton, N.J.: Princeton University Press, 1969.

• Romasco, Albert U. *The Politics of Recovery: Roosevelt's New Deal*. New York: Oxford University Press, 1983.

• Sitkoff, Harvard. *The Depression Decade*. Vol. 1 in *A New Deal for Blacks: The Emergence of Civil Rights as a National Issue*. Oxford, England: Oxford University Press, 1978.

• Ware, Susan. *Beyond Suffrage: Women in the New Deal*. Cambridge, Mass.: Harvard University Press, 1981.

supporters, who did not relish a breakdown in the separation of powers as advocated by the Framers of the Constitution (SEE Constitution of the U.S.). For Roosevelt, the court-packing plan became his greatest defeat of the New Deal era.

Other problems arose in 1937. Even though unemployment was still high and industrial productivity was relatively low, Roosevelt tried to end deficit spending by cutting the Public Works Administration and other programs. Social security reduced consumer income, and the Federal Reserve contracted the money supply. These factors led to a recession. In an attempt to end it, Roosevelt again turned to heavy federal deficit spending by 1938.

While the president called for no more major reforms to be made, Congress continued to pass legislation that was aimed at aiding farmers and workers. The Farm Security Administration helped tenants and sharecroppers to buy their own farms through loans while the Agricultural Adjustment Act of 1938 limited crop production and offered loans to farmers so that they could hold their crops until they had received a higher price for them.

Finally, the Fair Labor Standards Act banned child labor, set a minimum wage of $.40 per hour, and set a maximum work week of forty hours (SEE Fair Labor Standards Act). By January 1939 the New Deal had ended.

Stephen A. Berrey

Nez Perce Exile

SUMMARY

➤ In 1877 a group of Nez Perce in Oregon Territory were ordered to a reservation.
➤ They were preparing to leave peacefully, but on June 13 and 14 warriors killed four white men, and the tribe fled.
➤ The tribe fled for three months, engaging in battles with the troops several times.
➤ The tribe, forty miles away from Canada and safety, were attacked on September 30 and were forced to surrender on October 5.

The U.S. government, attempting to open more land for settlement, mining, and railroads, repeatedly pressured American Indians to sign treaties restricting them to small, defined areas (SEE Oregon Settlement; Westward Expansion). In 1863, Chief Joseph the Elder and his band of Nez Perce in the Oregon Territory did not join other Nez Perce in signing the latest treaty. They lived outside the treaty's boundaries without incident for many years because few settlers were interested in the area. In 1877, however, General Oliver Howard was sent to negotiate with the nontreaty Nez Perce, now led by Joseph's second son, Joseph the Younger. Ultimately, Howard ordered that the band move to the area delineated by the treaty within a month. Realizing that they

Chief Joseph of the Nez Perce tribe surrenders to Generals Miles and Howard at the Battle of Bear Paw Mountains on October 5, 1877. This defeat forced the Nez Perce into exile on reservations in Kansas and Oklahoma.

could not defeat the U.S. troops, Chief Joseph and other tribal leaders organized their people for the long trek across the Snake River to the designated reservation. The plan to leave peacefully was disrupted on June 13 and 14, when a few young warriors, emboldened by alcohol, killed four white men for whom they had a particular dislike. Ignoring Joseph's advice to plead that the tribe itself disapproved of the killings, the nontreaty Nez Perce turned and headed south, away from the reservation. One hundred cavalrymen were sent after them, but fifteen more settlers were killed before the troops could intercept the tribe.

On June 17, the Nez Perce tried to negotiate with the troops but were shot at by civilians who had joined the soldiers under the command of Captain David Perry. The Nez Perce, skilled horsemen and excellent shots, retaliated and killed thirty-three soldiers and one officer, sustaining no deaths. In response, General Howard gathered four hundred troops and civilians, hoping to trap Chief Joseph's band in White Bird Canyon. Part of Howard's force, led by Captain Stephen Whipple, was diverted to the nearby village of Chief Looking Glass, a Nez Perce who wanted to maintain neutrality. Whipple's plan to talk to the chief was subverted by the actions of the civilians. Looking Glass joined Chief Joseph's band in resisting the troops.

In early July, the Nez Perce bested troops and civilians in battles in the Cottonwood area. On July 11, Howard brought another force to attack the Nez Perce at Clearwater. Troops outnumbered the tribal warriors two to one, but the Nez Perce fought with skill and spirit, and although they lost the battle and were driven from the area, Howard's troops were unable to conclude the war. The Nez Perce escaped and proceeded east along the torturous Lolo Trail into Montana.

The next engagement was August 9 at the Big Hole River in Montana, where the Nez

CAUSES AND EFFECTS

U.S. agents significantly decreased the amount of land allotted to the Nez Perce, a group of autonomous Indian bands sharing the same language in the Oregon Territory. Some groups, known as treaty Indians, went to live on twenty-acre homesteads. Others, led by Chief Joseph the Elder, did not sign the treaty and insisted it did not bind them. In 1877, they were ordered to move to a reservation. After three months of fleeing and fighting, Chief Joseph the Younger and his group were sent to live on a reservation in Kansas, then in Oklahoma.

Although Chief Joseph won the respect of many in the federal government and was supported by both Colonel Nelson Miles and General Oliver Howard in his struggle to return his people to the Wallowa Valley, he was unable to regain what he considered to be their rightful land and died on the Colville Reservation in Washington.

Perce fought a force of two hundred, led by Colonel John Gibbon, to a draw. When the troops returned to their post, the Indians advanced 100 miles (160 kilometers) into Yellowstone National Park. The Nez Perces' success at Big Hole recalled Colonel George Custer's disastrous defeat at Little Bighorn a year earlier (see Battle of the Little Bighorn), causing fear among whites that a larger Indian uprising was being planned and generating criticism of Howard.

The Nez Perce were headed north through Montana to Canada, where they planned to join Sitting Bull, the renowned chief of the Hunkpapa Sioux, who had settled there with several thousand Sioux of

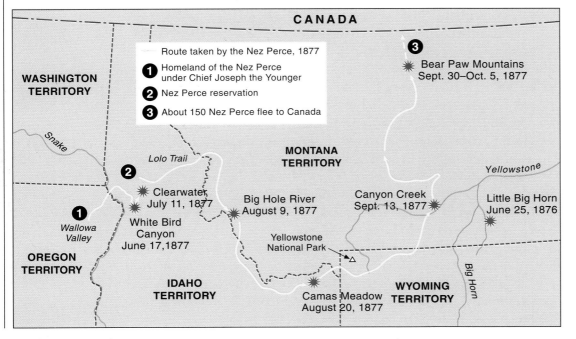

The Nez Perce were forced to leave their homeland in June 1877. After three months fighting and fleeing eastward across several states, they were finally defeated by U.S. troops.

PROFILE

CHIEF JOSEPH THE YOUNGER (C. 1840–1904)

Chief Joseph, known as Joseph the Younger to distinguish him from his father, Joseph the Elder, was born in the Wallowa Valley of Oregon. His Nez Perce name, Hin-mah-too-yah-lat-kekht, means "thunder rolling from the mountains." His father believed that embracing Christianity would help his people deal with the changing world and had his sons baptized. When Joseph the Elder died in 1871, Young Joseph and his brother Ollokot became the leaders of their tribal band: Ollokot led the men in hunts and battles, and Joseph was the camp chief, in charge of the seasonal moves from camp to camp and of representing the band in negotiations.

Chief Joseph's eloquent speech of surrender to Colonel Nelson Miles is one of the best-known speeches attributed to an American Indian: "I am tired of fighting. Our chiefs are killed. . . . My people, some of them, have run away to the hills and have no blankets, no food; no one knows where they are perhaps freezing to death. . . . I am tired; my heart is sick and sad. From where the sun now stands, I will fight no more, forever." Joseph had nine children, but only one survived until adulthood, and she died while still a young woman. Joseph spent the last years of his life raising horses, hunting, and serving as an advocate for his people to the U.S. government.

Chief Joseph of the Nez Perce tribe was devastated after his surrender at Bear Paw Mountains. He and his people had been pursued across several states. After the final defeat, Joseph lived peacefully.

SEE ALSO:
NORTHWEST COAST
INDIANS; OREGON
SETTLEMENT;
WESTWARD EXPANSION.

FURTHER READING
• Axelrod, Alan. *Chronicle of the Indian Wars: From Colonial Times to Wounded Knee.* New York: Prentice-Hall, 1993.
• Beal, Merrill D. *"I Will Fight No More Forever": Chief Joseph and the Nez Perce War.* Seattle: University of Washington Press, 1963.
• Lavender, David. *Let Me Be Free: The Nez Perce Tragedy.* New York: HarperCollins, 1992.
• Moeller, Bill, and Jan Moeller. *Chief Joseph and the Nez Perces: A Photographic History.* Missoula, Mont.: Mountain Press, 1995.

various bands after the Battle of Little Bighorn. Army troops futilely pursued the Nez Perce, unable to stop them in battles August 19-20 at the Camas Meadow near the Wyoming border or on September 13 in Canyon Creek near what is now Billings, Montana. However, the Nez Perce flight was impeded by an unanticipated enemy: Crow warriors associated with Colonel Samuel Sturgis, who had led the Seventh Cavalry at Canyon Creek. The Crow attacked and captured more than two hundred of the Nez Perce's horses, seriously crippling their mobility. Nevertheless, the Nez Perce pressed on toward Canada.

As the tribe wearied, Looking Glass, believing that the pursuing troops were farther behind than they actually were, decided to make camp temporarily in the Bear Paw Mountains, only forty miles outside of Canada. There, on September 30, nearly four hundred men led by Colonel Nelson Miles attacked the Nez Perce, beginning a bitter, six-day siege. Looking Glass and White Bird argued against surrender, but Chief Joseph favored it. On October 5, Chief Joseph surrendered to Colonel Miles, ending the three-month, seventeen-hundred-mile (twenty-seven-hundred-kilometer) journey.

About one hundred warriors and fifty women escaped with White Bird to Canada, but the rest of the Nez Perce were relocated to the Quapaw reservation in Kansas and then to Oklahoma. Neither the climate nor the accommodations at these reservations were appropriate for the Nez Perce, and many died. In 1885, after intense efforts by Chief Joseph, the Nez Perce were allowed to return to the Pacific Northwest—118 to the Lapwai reservation in Idaho and 150 to Colville in Washington.

Irene Struthers

Nicaraguan Civil War

Anastasio Somoza, who seized power in Nicaragua in 1933, created a family dynasty that lasted for forty-six years (SEE Somoza's Rule in Nicaragua). Somoza relied on U.S. support to maintain the regime, but because of apparent human-rights violations and corruption in the Nicaraguan government during the late 1970's, President James "Jimmy" Carter began to slowly withdraw U.S. support (SEE Carter's Presidency). Taking advantage of the opening, rebel groups united and managed to end Somoza's rule in 1979.

Soon after taking power, the rebels found that their political beliefs did not necessarily coincide. The largest of the groups, the Sandinista Front for National Liberation, or Sandinistas, led by Daniel Ortega, filled the most important positions in the government and began to reform Nicaragua with the goal of aiding the poor by distributing land and increasing the government's role in the economy. Because some Sandinistas were openly socialist, many Nicaraguans in the upper and middle classes feared the government was beginning to shift toward communism and approached the U.S. for assistance.

The election of Ronald Reagan, an anticommunist, to the presidency in 1980 signaled a shift in the U.S. government's attitude toward the Sandinistas from acceptance to strong opposition (SEE Reagan's Presidency). Soon after Reagan's election, Congress allocated money to increase the military forces of Nicaragua's neighbor, Honduras. After his inauguration in 1981, Reagan maintained the flow of money to Honduras while attacking the Nicaraguan economy, which had already been weakened by the war against Somoza. Reagan ended all American economic assistance to Nicaragua and blocked weapons shipments from Europe. The Sandinistas turned to Cuba and the Soviet Union for economic and military aid. Reagan viewed this action as a clear indication that the Sandinistas were communists and, in December, authorized the Central Intelligence Agency to spend nearly $20 million to gather, equip, and train

Supporters of the Sandinistas at a rally in Managua, Nicaragua, in 1980, a year after the organization seized control of the country.

counterrevolutionaries, or Contras, in Honduras to invade Nicaragua and remove the Sandinistas from power. For the next eight years, the U.S.-sponsored Contras engaged the Sandinistas in a fierce and destructive civil war as the Reagan administration simultaneously waged battle against the Nicaraguan economy.

In an effort to damage the Nicaraguan economy, the Contras burned huge sections of agricultural land and destroyed oil refineries, government buildings, and other parts of the country's infrastructure. The Reagan

SUMMARY

➢ Nicaraguan dictator Anastasio Somoza was overthrown in 1979 by a group of rebels, the Sandinistas, led by Daniel Ortega.
➢ President Ronald Reagan believed the Sandinistas to be communists and supported the Contras in their bid to overthrow the Sandinistas.
➢ In 1985, Lieutenant Colonel Oliver North agreed to exchange weapons for money with the Iranian government to aid the Contra cause, an act that became known as the Iran-Contra affair.
➢ In 1988, the Contras signed a cease-fire with the Sandinistas.

Lieutenant-Colonel Oliver North is sworn in before the House and Senate joint committee investigating the Iran-Contra affair.

administration continued its attack on the Nicaraguan economy by demanding that the World Bank and other international lending institutions discontinue providing aid to Nicaragua. The decrease in foreign aid and the boom in Contra attacks led the Sandinista government to impose stricter economic controls, which increased middle-class hostility toward the Sandinistas.

The decrease in upper- and middle-class support caused the government to turn to the lower classes to help fight the Contras. The

CAUSES AND EFFECTS

After Nicaraguan rebels ended the repressive Anastasio Somoza regime, the rebel alliance splintered. The leftist-leaning Sandinistas held most of the positions of power, and the Nicaraguan upper and middle classes, fearing the imposition of a harsh communist government, began to oppose the Sandinistas openly. The United States also opposed the forming of a possibly communist government in the Western Hemisphere and supported the efforts of the Contras, a counterrevolutionary group. The Nicaraguan civil war ended after the 1989 elections that removed the Sandinistas from power. The United States and the conservative elements of Nicaraguan society accepted the newly elected president, who was a member of the upper classes. Nearly immediately upon taking power, the president dismantled most of the Sandinistas' programs.

TEMPER OF THE TIMES

SANDINISTAS

Formed in 1961, the Sandinista Front for National Liberation, or Sandinistas, became the largest and most cohesive rebel group fighting the regime of Anastasio Somoza. The Sandinistas, who took their name from a well-known rebel of the 1920's, disliked not only the Somoza family's oppressive and corrupt rule but also the lack of an independent national policy. Some members were openly socialist, and when the Sandinistas dealt with the public, they emphasized their desire to improve the condition of the lower classes in the extremely poor country.

As the brutality and corruption of the Somoza family increased, the Sandinistas gained the support of more of the Nicaraguan population, even that of the Nicaraguan Catholic Church. In 1979, when it became increasingly obvious that Somoza was weakening, U.S. president James "Jimmy" Carter searched for an alternative to the Sandinistas, but when Somoza fell, the Sandinistas came to power. Once in power, the Sandinistas tried to aid the poor by opening the educational system to all Nicaraguans, distributing land to peasants, and creating a system of socialized medicine. In international issues, the Sandinistas voted as a bloc with other Third World countries, often canceling out the United States' vote.

Augusto Sandino, the guerrilla fighter of the 1920's whose name was adopted by the Sandinistas.

Sandinista army grew to 25,000 people, largely peasants, by the end of 1982. As the number of Contras swelled to 15,000 in 1983, the Nicaraguan government instituted a draft. The Sandinistas also offered amnesty to anyone who deserted the Contras, and over time, more and more Contras quit, especially after U.S. interest in Nicaragua began to wane.

As of 1984, however, the United States was still deeply involved. President Reagan ordered the U.S. Army to carry out unscheduled maneuvers in Honduras while the U.S. Navy ran drills off the coast. In response to the increased threat of invasion, the Sandinista army grew to its highest level of 40,000 soldiers.

Despite the immense economic strain caused by the civil war, the Sandinistas insisted on initiating the democratic process in Nicaragua and in 1984 held the first open elections in the country's history. Despite U.S. claims of electoral fraud, in late 1984, Ortega became the first democratically elected president in Nicaraguan history. Reagan responded by imposing a full trade embargo in 1985 and convincing Congress to send nearly $30 million in aid to the Contras. Later that year, in violation of a congressional amendment, National Security Council member Lieutenant Colonel Oliver North, working with the permission of the Reagan administration, agreed to exchange weapons for money with the Iranian government to aid the Contra effort. In 1986 the deal, which became known as the Iran-Contra affair, became public, dealing a severe blow to the Contra cause. Congressional investigation into the scandal ended future monetary packages and greatly limited CIA activities. Suffering from a drop in money, supplies, and training and the Nicaraguan government's amnesty program, the Contras signed a cease-fire with the Sandinistas in March 1988.

The civil war had, however, severely hurt the nation's already weak economy, causing $9 billion in damage and the deaths of 31,000 Nicaraguans in a country of four million people. In the 1989 elections, the Nicaraguans, tired of the violence and the pressure from the United States, elected a president who was not part of the Sandinista party. The new president, who was deemed politically acceptable by the United States, began to dismantle most of the social programs that the Sandinistas had attempted, but after eight years of civil war, Nicaragua was again at peace.

William Bridges

SEE ALSO:
CARTER'S PRESIDENCY;
NICARAGUAN
INDEPENDENCE;
NICARAGUAN
INTERVENTION;
REAGAN'S PRESIDENCY;
SOMOZA'S RULE IN
NICARAGUA.

FURTHER READING
•Booth, John A. *The End and the Beginning: The Nicaraguan Revolution.* 2d ed. Boulder, Colo.: Westview Press, 1985.
•Gutman, Roy. *Banana Diplomacy: The Making of American Policy in Nicaragua, 1981–1987.* New York: Simon & Schuster, 1988.
•Walker, Thomas W. *Nicaragua: The Land of Sandino.* 3d ed. Boulder, Colo.: Westview Press, 1991.
•_____, ed. *Revolution and Counterrevolution in Nicaragua.* Boulder, Colo.: Westview Press, 1991.

Nicaraguan Independence

Nicaragua, which gained independence from Spain in 1821, is a land of lush valleys and green hills.

CAUSES AND EFFECTS

Nicaraguan elites and merchants sought independence in an effort to free their economy from the restrictions of Spanish colonial rule. Eventually this desire for free trade, combined with a growing nationalism, spurred Nicaragua toward independence and self-government. Independence in Nicaragua resulted not in peace but in bloodshed. Liberal and conservative factions struggled for political control, culminating in a bloody civil war from 1821 to 1857 that not only destabilized the nation politically but also devastated Nicaragua economically.

SEE ALSO:
COSTA RICAN
INDEPENDENCE;
GUATEMALAN
INDEPENDENCE;
HONDURAN
INDEPENDENCE;
MEXICAN WAR OF
INDEPENDENCE;
SALVADORAN
INDEPENDENCE;
SPANISH COLONIAL
POLICIES; UNITED
PROVINCES OF
CENTRAL AMERICA.

Before Spanish conquistadors arrived in 1522, Nicaragua supported a population of approximately one million individuals from two distinct cultural groups. The people of the lowlands operated a relatively complex agricultural and trade-based society, and those in the highlands and Caribbean subsisted through hunting and gathering.

The arrival of the Spanish marked the start of three centuries of life as a colony for Nicaragua, a legacy that would fuel the political conflicts of the nation's future (SEE Spanish Colonial Policies). The people of Nicaragua first rebelled against colonial rule in 1811. Under Spanish rule, they suffered an enormous depletion of their population.

The colonizers exported indigenous Nicaraguans for the slave trade and inadvertently exposed them to European diseases, causing the native population to fall from one million to sixty thousand within sixty years. However, even these hardships did not incite revolution among the common people.

As in many other nations, the independence movement in Nicaragua began as an effort on the part of the elite and the merchant class to resist commercial taxes and restrictions imposed on colonial trade, then developed into a quest for self-determination and self-rule. Although the initial rebellion failed, in 1821 Nicaragua, along with Mexico and other nations in Central America, officially seceded from Spanish control (SEE Mexican War of Independence). After gaining their independence from Spain in 1821, Nicaragua, El Salvador, Guatemala, Honduras, and Costa Rica formed a federation called the United Provinces of Central America (SEE United Provinces of Central America). By 1823, Nicaragua had successfully freed itself from the control of Mexico as well. However, instead of generating political stability, independence in Nicaragua enabled factions within the nation to pursue internal power struggles.

The liberals sought to emulate the revolutions of the United States of America and the French republic and competed for control of the country with the conservatives, who fought to maintain the status quo. This conflict resulted in virtually constant civil war between 1821 and 1857, fighting that not only hampered political development in Nicaragua but also severely damaged its economy.

Margaret C. Gonzalez

Nicaraguan Intervention

U.S. marines in the firing line in support of U.S. interests during the Nicaraguan campaign of 1912.

In March 1912 the U.S. Secretary of State Philander Knox visited Nicaragua to bolster the image of the United States in that nation. Because of the growing resentment regarding U.S. control over Nicaraguan finances, Knox's visit was met by anti-American demonstrations in Managua on March 4 and 5.

Four months later, on July 29, this resentment resulted in nationalists under the leadership of the former president José Santos Zaleya revolting against the government. President Adolfo Díaz immediately requested help from Washington, D.C., to end the rebellion. On August 4, ninety-five American sailors arrived in Managua. As the revolt escalated, President William H. Taft ordered more U.S. troops into Nicaragua. By the end of August, more than three thousand sailors and U.S. Marines were stationed in the country.

The Marines and sailors were met by hostile demonstrations in León and Managua. These outbursts led to violent clashes in which several demonstrators were killed by U.S. forces. Various Central American nations, El Salvador in particular, protested the intervention and the contradictory nature of U.S. policy. Knox justified the involvement on the grounds that U.S. military personnel were there to protect American interests and to restore law and order to the country (see Monroe Doctrine).

By October, the insurrection had been put down at the cost of seven American lives. Martial law was declared, and a presidential election was held under the supervision of U.S. Marines. The only candidate in the race, American-backed Díaz, was reelected. The majority of U.S. troops were removed by the end of November, although one hundred Marines were left behind to deter any further outbreak of hostilities.

Charles T. Johnson

SEE ALSO:
DOLLAR DIPLOMACY;
MONROE DOCTRINE.

Nineteenth Amendment

A parade of suffragists in New York City during the early twentieth century as part of their ongoing campaign for equal rights for women.

SUMMARY

➤ In 1878, Susan B. Anthony submitted to Congress a constitutional amendment giving women the right to vote.
➤ When suffragists failed at the federal level, they concentrated on getting the vote in individual states.
➤ During World War I, Congress refused to consider a suffrage amendment, but President Woodrow Wilson agreed to support it in 1918.
➤ In 1919, the Nineteenth Amendment was ratified by the House and Senate.
➤ In 1920, the amendment was ratified by three-fourths of the state legislatures and became part of the Constitution.

A constitutional amendment that gave U.S. women the right to vote was first submitted to the U.S. Congress in 1878 by Susan B. Anthony. Suffragists lobbied for the amendment, which was opposed by members of the House and Senate, in each succeeding Congress until 1918 (SEE Woman Suffrage).

STATE-BY-STATE SUFFRAGE

After suffragists initially failed to get a federal amendment passed, they concentrated on winning the vote in individual states. State suffrage, they believed, would provide a model for the nation and lead to federal voting rights as women gained political influence. Their efforts paid off first in the more liberal Western states and territories. Wyoming granted women the vote in 1869, more than twenty years before any other territory or state; Colorado, Utah, and Idaho followed in the 1890's. After a series of defeats for suffragists, Western states again led the way in 1910 when Washington gave women the vote. Some states granted women partial suffrage in primary or presidential elections.

TWO IMPORTANT GROUPS

Two national organizations formed to lobby for voting rights: The American Woman Suffrage Association, which focused on winning the vote in individual states, and the more radical National Woman Suffrage Association, which worked to obtain a constitutional amendment. Although the organizations disagreed with each other's philosophy and tactics, when neither group met with considerable success they united to create the National American Woman Suffrage Association in 1890.

The association made slow progress, but as more states gave women the vote and more legislators became accountable to women, the possibility grew that Congress would be more receptive to a federal amendment. By 1920, the year the Nineteenth Amendment was passed, women had earned voting rights in thirty states.

GETTING HIGH-LEVEL SUPPORT

During World War I (1914–1918), despite women's dedicated service and contributions to the war effort, members of Congress refused to consider a suffrage amendment because they claimed it was not an emergency war measure. Militant suffragists marched, demonstrated, and picketed in front of the White House to demand that President Woodrow Wilson use his power to

CAUSES AND EFFECTS

The crusade for female suffrage gained momentum after passage of the Fifteenth Amendment, which gave African-American males, but not women, the right to vote. Members of the women's movement, who believed that winning the vote was the first step toward achieving other rights, made suffrage their main goal. Approximately eight million women voted in the November 1920 general election.

Although women had earned the right to vote, they still lacked political equality with men: Few women were elected to male-dominated legislatures. Women also continued to face discrimination in areas such as jobs and education. However, the amendment was the first important step on the gradual path toward gaining more equality in the following decades.

sway Congress on their behalf. The suffragists criticized Wilson for fighting to support democracy abroad while at the same time denying it to citizens at home in the United States (SEE Wilson's Presidency).

The suffragists threatened to campaign against Democrats in suffrage states if Congress and the president did not respond to their demands. Wilson also faced an outpouring of public sympathy after female protesters were arrested and jailed. Succumbing to the suffragists' threats and protests, the president finally agreed to support the women's cause.

In an address to Congress in 1918, Wilson urged the legislators to pass a suffrage amendment because it was "vitally essential" for winning the war: "We have made partners of the women in this war; shall we admit them only to a partnership of sacrifice and suffering and toil and not to a partnership of privilege and of right?"

Wilson's pleas, along with threats by women voters to oust Democratic legislators, convinced Congress to ratify the Nineteenth Amendment, but not without difficulty. Congress voted on the amendment eight times between 1887 and 1919. The last five votes were between January 1918 and June 1919. The House passed the amendment by the necessary two-thirds majority May 21, 1919; the Senate ratified the measure on June 4, 1919.

BATTLE FOR THE STATES

The fight for voting rights was not over after congressional ratification: The amendment would not become part of the Constitution until three-fourths of the state legislatures—thirty-six out of forty-eight—ratified the measure. The suffragists, who encountered an

uphill battle for state ratification, employed the same persistent lobbying strategies they had used to persuade Congress. Wisconsin was the first state to adopt the amendment,

A poster for the Woman's Land Army in World War I, when women worked on equal basis with men.

FURTHER READING
•Ford, Linda G. *Iron-Jawed Angels: The Suffrage Militancy of the National Woman's Party, 1912–1920.* Lanham, Md.: University Press of America, 1991.
•Kraditor, Aileen. *The Ideas of the Woman Suffrage Movement, 1890–1920.* New York: W. W. Norton, 1981.
•Stevens, Doris. *Jailed for Freedom: American Women Win the Vote.* Edited by Carol O'Hare. Troutdale, Oreg.: NewSage Press, 1995.
•Wheeler, Marjorie Spruill, ed. *One Woman, One Vote: Rediscovering the Woman Suffrage Movement.* Troutdale, Oreg.: NewSage Press, 1995.

PROFILE

ALICE PAUL (1885–1977)

Alice Paul was born to a Quaker family in New Jersey and educated at Swarthmore College, the University of Pennsylvania, and the London School of Economics. In England, she became active in the militant British women's suffrage movement. After returning to the United States, Paul joined the National American Woman Suffrage Association (NAWSA) in 1912. As chair of the organization's congressional committee, her goal was to secure a women's voting amendment to the Constitution. In March 1913, on the day before Woodrow Wilson took the presidential oath of office, Paul organized a parade that stirred public sympathy for the suffrage cause when police failed to protect the marchers from harassment by onlookers.

In 1914 Paul broke ranks with the more conservative members of the NAWSA, who disapproved of her militant style and her stubborn stance that the party in power was responsible for women's not getting the vote, and formed the National Woman's Party. Under Paul's leadership, members of the group were the first Americans to picket the White House for a political cause. Even after the ratification of the Nineteenth Amendment, Paul believed women would not achieve full equality until a constitutional amendment was passed that guaranteed them equal rights with men. In 1923 she wrote and submitted to Congress the Equal Rights Amendment.

American feminist Alice Paul raises a toast at a women's rally. Paul authored the first equal rights amendment considered by Congress.

in June 1919. Other Western states where women already had the right to vote were next to ratify the measure.

The drive for ratification progressed slowly, but by the summer of 1920 the suffragists needed only one more state to achieve the necessary thirty-six. No more legislative sessions were scheduled before the next election, but the president convinced the Democratic governors of North Carolina and Tennessee to convene special sessions. When North Carolina failed to ratify the amendment, the final showdown moved to the Tennessee legislature.

After considerable political maneuvering and delaying tactics on the part of antisuffragist legislators in the House, a final vote was taken. The deciding vote was cast by the legislature's youngest member, twenty-four-year-old Harry Burn.

The previously undecided Burn broke a possible tie—the final vote was 49 to 47—by following his mother's admonishment to vote for the amendment. Despite attempts by antisuffragist legislators to delay or reconsider ratification, the Nineteenth Amendment was officially proclaimed by the secretary of state August 26, 1920.

The amendment reads: "The right of citizens of the United States to vote shall not be denied or abridged by the United States or by any State on account of sex. Congress shall have power to enforce this article by appropriate legislation."

Karen Lindell

Nixon's Presidency

Richard Nixon was elected president of the United States in 1968 with only a plurality of the popular vote (43.3 percent) in a close three-way race with Democrat Hubert Humphrey (42.7 percent) and American Independent George Wallace (13.5 percent). The political divisions over the Vietnam War and the struggle for African-American equality in the face of white resistance led to this close result and dominated the Nixon years.

SUPREME COURT APPOINTMENTS

Domestically, Nixon's presidency was dominated by the continuing civil-rights controversy (SEE Civil Rights Movement). This struggle was manifested in Nixon's appointments to the Supreme Court. Nixon's longest-lasting impact arguably came from his opportunity to appoint four U.S. Supreme Court justices in his five-and-one-half years as president. Only three other presidents—Benjamin Harrison, William Howard Taft, and Warren Harding—appointed as many justices while serving such a short time.

Nixon's early appointments of Minnesotan Warren Burger to replace retiring Chief Justice Earl Warren and of Minnesotan Harry Blackmun to take the place of scandal-plagued Abe Fortas engendered little controversy. However, when Nixon attempted to fulfill a campaign promise made to southern supporters by appointing a southerner to the Court, he failed twice in a row.

Southerner Clement Haynesworth, an otherwise distinguished U.S. Court of Appeals judge, was rejected after being accused of continuing to sit on a case involving a corporation in which he owned stock. Nixon followed by nominating Federal District Judge G. Harold Carswell, who was rejected for having had a high level of reversals by higher courts, for having been a member of an all-white country club, and for having made pro-segregation remarks in speeches early in his political career. Nixon finally succeeded in naming a southerner to the Court when he chose a distinguished moderate Democrat from Virginia, Louis

Richard Nixon was beaten narrowly in the 1960 presidential election by John F. Kennedy, but in 1968 Nixon ran again and was elected the 37th president of the United States.

Powell, to fill the vacancy. Later, Nixon successfully appointed conservative William Rehnquist to the Court. Nixon thus had an unusually large impact on the Supreme Court's character.

FOREIGN AFFAIRS

The Vietnam War dominated politics at the time, and Nixon's fundamental policy rested on a disengagement of U.S. forces from Vietnam (SEE Military Draft; Vietnam War). During the 1968 campaign, he had promised to end the war in Vietnam. To hawks, or supporters of the Vietnam War, he implied that he planned to use stronger military

SUMMARY

➤ Richard Nixon was elected president of the United States in 1968 in a close three-way race with Democrat Hubert Humphrey and American Independent George Wallace.

➤ Nixon's presidency was dominated by divisions over the Vietnam War and civil-rights issues.

➤ The civil-rights issue manifested itself in controversies over two of Nixon's four appointees to the Supreme Court.

➤ He succeeded in improving relations with the Soviet Union and the People's Republic of China but was unable to pressure the Vietnamese into accepting a negotiated settlement.

➤ Nixon did bring the war to a close, but only after heavy bombing of North Vietnam.

President Nixon and his family arrive for the New York caucus in 1972, during his third presidential campaign. America supported his reelection, but he resigned office in 1974.

action to win the war. To doves, or people who wanted to end the war, he implied that he planned peace negotiations to disengage from Vietnam without achieving a victory.

With Harvard professor (and later secretary of state) Henry Kissinger as his National Security Council adviser, Nixon devised a plan for détente, or lessened tensions, with the Soviet Union (SEE U.S.-Soviet Détente)

and rapprochement with the previously isolated People's Republic of China (SEE Rapprochement with China), the two major allies of North Vietnam, which was fighting the U.S.-backed South Vietnam.

Though Nixon succeeded in improving relations with the Soviet Union and China, he did not achieve his principal goal of pressuring the North Vietnamese into

CAUSES AND EFFECTS

The political divisions over the Vietnam War and civil rights seriously weakened Lyndon Johnson's Democratic administration. In the 1968 presidential race, Vice President Hubert Humphrey, who took Johnson's place as Democratic nominee of a badly split party, fought from far back in the polls to within a few hundred thousand votes of the Republican winner, Richard Nixon. Nixon could not easily take advantage of the Democratic split because the third alternative, George Wallace, though a Democratic governor, was a racial conservative who took some votes away from both the conservative Nixon and the more liberal Humphrey.

Elected president of a badly divided nation with a minority of the popular vote and faced with a Congress in which Democrats controlled both houses, Nixon recognized he would not be reelected if the Democrats united in the 1972 election campaign. In the face of ongoing criticism by antiwar protesters and what he perceived as the liberal media, he developed a siege mentality that included a willingness to bend or break laws, if necessary, to divide the opposition. The Democratic nominee, George McGovern, proved to be a weak candidate whom Nixon easily defeated in a landslide, but the Nixon campaign's excesses included the fatefully destructive Watergate burglary.

VIEWPOINTS

NIXON'S VICTORIES

President Richard Nixon's positive achievements included rapprochement with the People's Republic of China and reduction of tensions between the two nuclear superpowers under the U.S.-Soviet détente policy. Both initiatives supported U.S. efforts to influence North Vietnam's two most important allies and bring about a settlement of the Vietnam War favorable to the United States. Although these initiatives failed, U.S. military forces in Vietnam were reduced, easing domestic tensions somewhat, and one year after his reelection in 1972, the Vietnam War did come to an end with the signing of a peace treaty in Paris.

Domestically, Nixon can be credited with the creation of the Environmental Protection Agency and with general revenue sharing as an alternative to excessively restrictive categorical grants to states and cities. He also signed into law the Equal Employment Opportunity Act of 1972, which dramatically increased the authority of the Equal Employment Opportunity Commission to enforce civil rights-laws against discrimination in the workplace.

Richard Nixon in Peking on his "journey of peace" in 1972, during which he forged economic and diplomatic ties with China.

a ground invasion of Cambodia to defeat the Vietnamese militarily (SEE Cambodia Invasion). Neither materially shortened the war nor avoided ultimate North Vietnamese success. Nevertheless, after repeated breakdowns in negotiations and finally renewed U.S. bombing of North Vietnam, a peace accord was signed January 31, 1973.

NIXON'S FALL

The Vietnam War had provoked repeated antiwar demonstrations on college campuses and in the streets of Washington, D.C. Though the antiwar movement and the Civil Rights movement were separate, there was substantial overlap in their philosophy, and they both directed their protests toward the Nixon administration. The depth of their opposition produced a kind of siege mentality in the Nixon administration, leading to the creation of the so-called plumber's unit responsible for the Watergate affair and ultimately Nixon's resignation from the presidency (SEE Watergate Affair). In 1974, Richard Nixon became the first president ever to resign under the threat of impending impeachment.

Richard L. Wilson

accepting a favorable settlement. Such agreements as were negotiated were in a large part driven by the U.S. disengagement from a losing military effort: As China perceived the United States to be moving toward a withdrawal from Vietnam, it was motivated to engage in détente as a means of solidifying its international position.

This U.S. Vietnam policy used a carrot-and-stick approach, offering the North Vietnamese the "carrot" of a negotiated eventual withdrawal of U.S. forces if they reduced their military effort and the "stick" of increased bombing of North Vietnam and

SEE ALSO:
CAMBODIA INVASION; CHICAGO RIOTS; EISENHOWER'S PRESIDENCY; JOHNSON'S PRESIDENCY; MILITARY DRAFT; RAPPROCHEMENT WITH CHINA; ROE V. WADE; U.S.-CHINESE RELATIONS; U.S.-SOVIET DÉTENTE; VIETNAM WAR; WATERGATE AFFAIR; WELFARE REFORM.

FURTHER READING
•Genovese, Michael A. *The Nixon Presidency.* New York: Greenwood Press, 1990.
•Safire, William. *Before the Fall: An Inside View of the Pre-Watergate White House.* Garden City, N.Y.: Doubleday, 1975.
•Sussman, Barry. *The Great Cover-up: Nixon and the Scandal of Watergate.* Arlington, Va.: Seven Locks Press, 1992.
•White, Theodore E. *Breach of Faith: The Fall of Richard Nixon.* New York: Atheneum, 1975.
•Wicker, Tom. *One of Us: Richard Nixon and the American Dream.* New York: Random House, 1991.

Nootka Sound Convention

Britain's Captain George Vancouver met with Spain's Captain Juan Bodega y Quadra to discuss property transfers on Nootka in 1792. The issue was resolved in 1795 when Nootka Sound was abandoned by both Spain and Britain, and left open to international trade.

CAUSES AND EFFECTS

During the seventeenth and eighteenth centuries, the Spanish and British competed for the maritime fur trade in the Pacific Northwest. The two countries' disregard for property rights at Nootka Sound caused a diplomatic crisis that was settled by the creation of the Nootka Sound Convention in 1790.

When Spain conceded exclusive sovereignty on the Pacific Northwest coast, its influence rapidly faded in the area. By 1795, British and American merchants dominated the Nootka trade.

SEE ALSO:
NORTHWEST COAST
INDIANS; PACIFIC
TRADE ROUTES.

Nootka Sound, located on the west coast of Vancouver Island, offers one of the finest natural harbors in the Pacific Northwest. Both Spain and Great Britain asserted claims to the sound and its lucrative Nootka Indian fur trade based on the 1774 voyage of Juan Pérez and the 1778 voyage of James Cook.

In 1788, English mariner John Meares ordered the construction of a trading hut at Nootka Sound. Meares departed, but his workers remained. In June 1789, Esteban José Martínez formally claimed the area by establishing a Spanish garrison.

Shortly thereafter, four ships representing Meares' interests arrived to build a permanent trading post. Martínez promptly seized three of the vessels and their crews when they refused to leave and destroyed the British trading hut. The Spaniards took two of the ships and crews to Mexico and proceeded to sail the third ship in the Pacific Northwest under the Spanish flag.

News of the seizures reached Europe in January 1790. Britain demanded the return of all British property, including ships and land; the freedom of the crews; $210,000 for the hut; Spanish renunciation of claims to California; and the reception of British merchants throughout the Spanish empire.

The Spanish insisted on the legality of its sovereign actions at Nootka, but crises in Europe surrounding the French Revolution weakened Spanish resolve. The Spanish and British agreed on a compromise, the Nootka Sound Convention, in October 1790, stipulating that Spain pay the indemnity, release British property and crew members, and open the coast of the Pacific Northwest to trade (SEE Pacific Trade Routes).

Britain's Captain George Vancouver and Spain's Captain Juan Bodega y Quadra met at Nootka in 1792 to oversee the transfer of property. Vancouver understood that Britain should receive all of Nootka; however, Bodega y Quadra sought to return only the land on which the hut stood. The two men diplomatically referred the matter back to their respective governments.

In the meantime, Spain retained sovereignty at Nootka as British and American merchants continued plying the area's trade. Britain and Spain reached another agreement on Nootka in 1794. The following year, a joint British-Spanish commission sailed to Nootka, raised and lowered the Union Jack, and both countries abandoned the sound, leaving it open to international trade.

Ken Zontek

North Atlantic Treaty

On April 4, 1949, in Washington, D.C., four years after the end of World War II, tensions arose between the Soviet Union and the Western Allies. Prompted by the creation of communist dictatorships in Eastern Europe and the 1948 Berlin Blockade, the North Atlantic Treaty created the North Atlantic Treaty Organization (NATO). NATO provided for the collective defense of Europe from a Soviet attack. Signatory powers to the treaty were France, Great Britain, Belgium, the Netherlands, Luxembourg, Canada, Denmark, Portugal, Norway, Iceland, Italy, and the U.S. General Dwight D. Eisenhower was appointed NATO's first supreme allied commander.

The North Atlantic Council, composed of the foreign ministers of member nations and located in Brussels, Belgium, served as the coordinating body for NATO with a military committee based in Washington, D.C. Turkey and Greece joined the alliance in 1952, the Federal Republic of Germany (West Germany) in 1955. In 1967, France pulled its military forces out of NATO but retained its membership.

In 1955, the Soviet Union countered NATO by establishing the Warsaw Pact, which included Albania, Bulgaria, Czechoslovakia, the German Democratic Republic (East Germany), Poland, and Romania. By 1989, NATO's position in Europe had changed dramatically after the collapse of the Soviet Union and the end of the Cold War. In 1990, NATO and the Warsaw Pact signed an agreement to greatly reduce conventional military forces. NATO's future was redefined to include a smaller role for the United States and the possibility of extending membership to former Warsaw Pact nations with the objective of evolving into a security organization covering all of Europe. Russia announced its decision not to join NATO in May 1997, however, the organization invited Poland, the Czech Republic, and Hungary to join in July 1997. Controversy continued to swirl around the roles that NATO should play, its finances, and the levels of military preparedness it should maintain.

V. M. Leslie

Three members of a NATO aircrew—a German, Canadian, and American—cooperate aboard an E–3A AWACS early-warning aircraft during military exercises.

CAUSES AND EFFECTS

After World War II, the creation of the Soviet bloc, which established Soviet domination over much of central and eastern Europe, brought about a decline in relations between the Soviet Union and the Western Allies. This decline prompted many of the Allies to sign the North Atlantic Treaty and to create a military alliance, the North Atlantic Treaty Organization (NATO), chiefly aimed at the defense of Europe.

The Soviet Union responded by creating the Warsaw Pact, made up of central and eastern European countries. The uneasy balance between NATO and the Warsaw Pact helped maintain peace in the era of the Cold War. NATO contributed to the eventual collapse of the Soviet Union. Following the breakup of the Soviet Union, NATO's future became tied to the drive toward European unification.

SEE ALSO:
BERLIN BLOCKADE;
COLD WAR;
EISENHOWER'S
PRESIDENCY; U.S.-
SOVIET DÉTENTE;
WORLD WAR II IN
EUROPE.

North Pole Expeditions

Robert Edwin Peary plants the Stars and Stripes during an Arctic expedition made during 1906.

One of the most dedicated explorers of the nineteenth century was Robert Edwin Peary, a civil engineer in the U.S. Navy. At age fifty-three and after seven previous Arctic expeditions between 1886 and 1908, Peary presumably was the first to reach the North Pole, a feat that he claimed to have accomplished on April 6, 1909, with four Inuit and his resourceful and talented companion Matthew Henson, an African-American who spoke fluent Inuit.

The expedition, sponsored by the National Geographic Society, was taken to the north head of Baffin Bay by Captain Robert Bartlett in the steam-powered *Roosevelt*. Bartlett transported the explorers, fifty Inuit, nineteen sledges, and 250 sledge dogs to the edge of the pack ice and broke trail to within 150 miles (242 kilometers) of the North Pole while the lame Peary followed on a sledge pulled by Inuit. At 87°47' north latitude, Peary, Henson, and four Inuit staged a final assault on the point they believed was the North Pole. Despite Peary's experience, knowledge, and extensive use of Inuit techniques of survival, many critics doubt that he really reached the North Pole, believing it impossible that he actually traveled forty-four miles (seventy-one kilometers) a day, a distance that no Arctic explorer had ever accomplished, including the renowned sledger Roald Amundsen. Also, Peary's nineteenth-century handheld navigational devices and techniques meant he had to use dead reckoning, an imprecise method of navigation. Peary is also faulted for not making longitudinal observations.

John Alan Ross

CAUSES AND EFFECTS

By the beginning of the twentieth century and with the rise of nationalism, most regions of the world had been explored. Only the South and North Poles and the elusive Arctic Northwest Passage remained unmapped. After the great Antarctic and Arctic explorer Roald Amundsen discovered the Northwest Passage in the early 1900's, many countries and even individuals sought to claim the North Pole.

Robert Edwin Peary's claim to have been the first to reach the North Pole was publicly refuted by Frederick Cook, who said he had reached the Pole on April 21, 1908, a claim cast into doubt by the fact that his earlier assertion that he had been the first to ascend Mount McKinley in 1906 later proved fraudulent. Later, Arctic and navigational scholars concluded that Peary was approximately thirty to sixty miles (fifty to one hundred kilometers) short of his goal, and that neither he nor Cook was the first to reach the North Pole.

Index

Page numbers in **bold** refer to full articles; those in *italics* refer to illustrations and their captions.